Instrumental Social Justice in Higher Education

"This book provides rich and thoughtful guidance on the design and implementation of survey instruments as well as the data analysis and communication of the findings to inform and facilitate meaningful social action. Hollis' storytelling approach uniquely captures and highlights the dynamic and evolving process of the research and the researcher and the intimate connection between the two; how they shape each other. An incredible and rare combination of technical information, numbers, and lived experienced woven in a single text."
—Loraleigh Keashly, Professor, *Department of Communication, Distinguished Service Professor, Wayne State University, USA*

"What an informative and rich resource for anyone who is looking at the main causality of the current lack of social justice in higher education. Through the need for development of more robust consideration of qualitative research design and implementation of studies in social justice, this book provides a unique opportunity for the relevant communities (including minorities) to substantially improve their study design, data collection, analysis, and reporting. Such robust and accurate outcomes of qualitative studies enable policy makers and gatekeepers to develop timely and effective strategies to substantially improve social justice for everyone."
—Morteza Mahmoudi, *Associate Professor at Michigan State University, USA and Co-Founder and Director of the Academic Parity Movement*

"Hollis takes social justice to the next level by examining how quantitative research can be more accessible for everyone. Her thought-provoking question asking why we don't see more people of color doing quantitative research is an important one. She expertly makes her work intersectional and accessible. People interested in pursuing quantitative research in general and workplace bullying scholarship in particular will benefit from the insights provided in this book."
—Stacy Tye-Williams, *Associate Professor of Communication Studies/English at Iowa State University, USA*

Leah P. Hollis

Instrumental Social Justice in Higher Education

Eight Surveys for Workplace Bullying and Social Justice Research

Leah P. Hollis
Equity, Access, and Inclusion
College of Education The Pennsylvania State University
University Park, PA, USA

ISBN 978-3-031-49288-4   ISBN 978-3-031-49289-1   (eBook)
https://doi.org/10.1007/978-3-031-49289-1

Cover illustration: Pattern © Melisa Hasan

This Palgrave Macmillan imprint is published by the registered company Springer Nature
Switzerland AG.
The registered company address is: Gewerbestrasse 11, 6330 Cham, Switzerland

Paper in this product is recyclable.

Contents

LIST OF FIGURES

LIST OF TABLES

CHAPTER 1

Foreword

Abstract The foreword explains the motivation for this book. Too often, research methods are racialized and assigned to various racial groups based on myths propagated by early mathematicians. Those of European descent often align with quantitative methods, while qualitative methods often align with critical race research and studies about disenfranchised populations. However, history shows that mathematical reasons originated from Africa, then co-oped by the Greeks. The miseducation that reflects the erroneous and inaccurate origin of math disenfranchises many Black and brown scholars who have been told that math, statistics, and quantitative reasoning is for and by European scholars. However, when legislatures make policies and create laws, they often rely on research from large samples; such large sample sizes tend to support quantitative research. Hence, this Foreword provides detailed information about the origins of math.

Quantitative reasoning is not the master's tools but tools and logic that initially emerged from the African and South American continents.

Keywords Ethnomathematics • Nazca Lines • Pythagorean theorem • Math origins

L. P. Hollis, *Instrumental Social Justice in Higher Education*, https://doi.org/10.1007/978-3-031-49289-1_1

Too often I attend academic conferences for educational research that offer wonderful presentations, yet precious few include scholars of color using quantitative research methods. While I respect and conduct qualitative research myself, I know firsthand that quantitative methods seem to be more accepted for policy development. Such methods rely on large samples and predictive statistics models such as multiple regression and chi-square. With the struggle for racial and gender-based equity, social justice scholars are needed to research with the critical race and womanist lenses at the foundation of quantitative analysis.

Additionally, educational research highlights the difficulty many Black and brown people have with math (Shah, 2019; Trytten et al., 2012). While such deficits in math performance are discernible, history shows that mathematical reason was at the root of several cultures. Earlier civilizations, many emerging from Africa and South America, were at the inception of math, medicine, and statistics (Walker & Matthews, 2014). For example, 37,000 years ago, Namibians used the Lebombo Bone to monitor moon phases and time. In 2011, Setati and Bangura confirmed that mathematical reasoning occurred with the Moors and was found in Egyptian hieroglyphics. Institutions of higher learning in Katsina and Timbuktu taught mathematical reasoning, with Aristotle crediting Egypt as the "cradle of mathematical arts" (Walker & Matthews, 2014).

Agrarian societies throughout Africa and South America used math to manage crops and evaluate constellations. Such advanced math is at the root of the geometry and algebra, which led to the great pyramids in Egypt and the lost pyramids in the Sudan. Similarly, pre-Colombian cultures in what is now Mexico used math to develop Chichén Itzá, a large pyramid that uses the angle of the sun on the fall and spring equinoxes to reveal the shadow of a large snake (Scalisi & Fairbanks, 2005). In the same vicinity, the ancient Mayans built the Caracol (Snail) Observatory in AD 800 to track the stars. During their rule from 500 BC to AD 1500, they also built the Temple of Seven Dolls, which used the sun during the fall and spring equinoxes to confirm the beginning of new seasons. As Diel (2018) noted, the Aztec Tonalpohualli calendar was the sacred calendar, while this Mesoamerican culture used a xiuhpohualli solar calendar to record events:

> The system of the tonalpohualli can be best understood by imagining two wheels that are connected to each other. One wheel has the numbers "one"

to "thirteen" written on it. The second wheel has twenty symbols on it. In the initial situation, number "one" combines with the first symbol. This is the first day of the tonalpohualli. Now the wheels start moving and number "two" combines with the second glyph. This is the second day. After fourteen days, an Aztec week (trecena in Spanish) of thirteen days has passed. The wheel with the numbers shows the number "one" again. The other wheel now shows the fourteenth symbol. After 260 days, the two wheels have returned to their initial position. The tonalpohualli starts all over again. (French, 2017, p. 26)

Ancient Egyptian records show that Africans were using mathematical proofs in agriculture and industry. Records show that Africans were using math in industry, medicine, and agriculture. After wartime, they used math to manage animals and foodstuff acquired in battle.

Statistical games and gambling games served as a rite of passage for the Kuna Kingdom. Just as the Congolese had such games to test intelligence, the Songhai Empire also had a game that replicated chess. The Ibo (also known as Igbo) tribe were intellectually advanced in math and linguistics (Chisala, 2015; Umeh, 1998). Just north is Benin, which also incorporated math into their textiles (Crowe, 1975).

Other researchers confirm that Angolan culture used math to develop algorithms and topography. Topographical talent is also evident in the symmetrical Nazca Lines of animals and insects that Peruvian indigenous people created in South America. Through math, this indigenous population created symmetrical large-scale drawings that can be seen only from the sky, yet the pictures were symetric despite the scale. Mardon (2021) reported that such lines, or geoglyphs, were as large as 50 square kilometers. Researchers have not confirmed exactly the geoglyphs' purpose (Briones, 2006). With over 1170 lines carved into the desert floor (Mardon, 2021), some suggest it is simply an art, while others speculate it is part of an irrigation system in the desert, for some astrological purpose, or guidance for travelers (Briones, 2006; Mendoza, 2019). Regardless of the purpose, the scale and symmetry signify advanced mathematical reasoning.

These early cultures were at the inception of the Pythagorean theorem that emerged from African cultures, while other African cultures in Ethiopia, the Congo, Djenne, Mali, Songhai, and Zimbabwe used math daily (Walker & Matthews, 2014). Additionally, the Yoruba people had a counting system that remained in use for over four centuries (Zaslavsky,

1973). Like other aforementioned tribes, Ethiopia also had math-related games dating from 700 BC.

Despite the rich history of Africans and pre-Colombian Americans having a substantial mathematical background that was at the inception of multiple cultures, contemporary students from African and Hispanic diasporas seem to have a minor presence in statistical reasoning for modern social science research. Descendants of African and Latin cultures at times have math anxiety, and in turn do not engage strong mathematical reasoning (de Carvalho, 2013; Fernández et al., 2021); Hall et al., 1999). This results in fewer students from the African and Latin diasporas pursuing math in college (Lawrence et al., 2010). Though these communities have been told, and at times embrace, that math and statistics are the product of current dominant cultures, mathematical and statistical reasoning are necessary processes to research social justice and create viable policies. However, when communities of color are dissuaded from math and statistics, other scholars are positioned to conduct the analysis and yield policy that may not truly assist these communities (Kaye & Aickin, 1986). The battle for equal rights is supported with statistical trends and benchmarks proving that math and statistics are viable tools in establishing disparate impact, jury selection, and a host of unconstitutional acts. Arguably, communities of color need to re-embrace statistical and mathematical reasoning in greater numbers to have more direct influence in the policy development that impacts these communities.

References

Briones, M. L. (2006). The geoglyphs of the north Chilean desert: An archaeological and artistic perspective. *Antiquity, 80*(307), 9–24.

Chisala, C. (2015). The IQ gap is no longer a black and white issue. The Unz Review. A collection of interesting, important, and controversial perspectives largely excluded from the American mainstream media. www.unz.com/article/the-iq-gap-is-no-longer-a-black-and-white-issue/

Crowe, D. (1975). Geometry of African art: A catalogue of Benin patterns. *Historia Mathematica., 2*, 253–1711.

de Carvalho, J. B. P. (2013). Mathematics education in Latin America. *Handbook on the History of Mathematics Education*, 335–359.

Diel, L. B. (2018). A history of the Mexica people: From Aztlan to Tenochtitlan to New Spain. In L. B. Diel (Ed.), *The Codex Mexicanus a guide to life in late sixteenth-century New Spain*. University of Texas Press. https://doi.org/10.7560/316733

Fernández, L. M., Wang, X., Ramirez, O., & Villalobos, M. C. (2021). Latinx Students' Mathematics Anxiety and Their Study Habits: Exploring Their Relationship at the Postsecondary Level. *Journal of Hispanic Higher Education, 20*(3), 278–296.

French, C. (2017). Patterns around the world: Japanese, Maori, Islamic, Aztec/ Mayan, African. *Curricula, 25.* https://scholarworks.lib.csusb.edu/cap-curr/25

Hall, C. W., Davis, N. B., Bolen, L. M., & Chai, R. (1999). Gender and racial differences in mathematical performance. *The Journal of Social Psychology, 139*(6), 677–689.

Kaye, D. H., & Aickin, M. (1986). *Statistical methods in discrimination litigation.* Taylor & Francis Group.

Lawrence, J. S., Marks, B. T., & Jackson, J. S. (2010). Domain identification predicts black students' underperformance on moderately-difficult tests. *Motivation and Emotion, 34*(2), 105–109. https://doi.org/10.1007/s11031-010-9159-8

Mardon, A. (2021). *The Nazca lines.* Golden Meteorite Press.

Mendoza, A. M. C. (2019, June 4). The Nazca lines: A life's work. World History Encyclopedia.   https://www.worldhistory.org/article/1395/ the-nazca-lines-alifes-work/

Scalisi, P., & Fairbanks, P. (2005). A Mathematical Journey through the Land of the Maya. *Bridgewater Review, 24*(2), 8–13.

Setati, M., & Bangura, A. K. (2011). *African mathematics: From bones to computers.* UPA Acquisitions Department.

Shah, N. (2019). "Asians are good at math" is not a compliment: STEM success as a threat to personhood. *Harvard Educational Review, 89*(4), 661–686, 702.

Trytten, D. A., Lowe, A. W., & Walden, S. (2012). "Asians are good at math. What an awful stereotype": The model minority stereotype's impact on Asian American engineering students. *Journal of Engineering Education* (Washington, DC), *101*(3), 439–468. Electronic Copy Available at: https://ssrn.com/ abstract=414046111 https://doi.org/10.1002/j.2168-9830.2012.tb00057.x

Umeh, A. (1998). *After God is Dibia.* Africa World Press.

Walker, R., & Matthews, J. (2014). *African mathematics: History, textbook and classroom.* Reklaw Education.

Zaslavsky, C. (1973). Mathematics in the study of African culture. *The Arithmetic Teacher, 20*(7), 532–535.

CHAPTER 2

The Art of Social Justice Research: Creating and Validating Instruments for Workplace Bullying Research

Abstract This book is designed for social justice minded scholars who might have an original love for qualitative research, language, interviews, and coding. As I tell my doctoral students, qualitative methods are not harder than quantitative methods; the converse is true. Quantitative methods are not harder than qualitative. They are different and bring different issues, all of which can be transcended with enough grit and determination.

To give the reader context, I majored in English Literature and Africana Studies at a time that "Black Studies" was not wholly embraced. It was considered a "nice" second major. Since that time, starting with Dr. Molefi Asante's inaugural doctoral program in Black Studies at Temple University, several colleges and universities have also embraced the value of ethnic studies doctoral programs [Karenga, *Journal of Black Studies*, 49(6), 576–603 (2018)], Cornell University, Penn State University, University of Texas-Austin, and Yale University, to name a few.

Since the 2022 AERA conference in San Diego, I found myself wondering why more BiPOC scholars did not embrace statistics. I asked my mentors and colleagues, who have noticed the same phenomena. It left me asking, where are the Blacks in Stats? Then I thought of what we know about student development along racial, gendered, and socio-economic lines.

L. P. Hollis, *Instrumental Social Justice in Higher Education*, https://doi.org/10.1007/978-3-031-49289-1_2

Women are typically ostracized in the STEM fields and find such environments uncomfortable. When I reflect on my own math history, I originally loved algebra. I had a wonderful teacher who crisscrossed the building in her red clogs and blonde hair. She was accessible to boys and girls, leaving all of us liking math. Yet my math journey wavered when I had a male teacher for calculus. I found him to be dismissive and belittling. I did not like the class and focused more on subjects that brought greater rewards, such as being accepted by the teacher.

I grappled again with math and statistics in my doctoral program and found that the research questions I had were not qualitative. My research pursued predictive models such as "what services truly serve student athlete graduation rates" [Hollis, *Equal opportunity for student-athletes: Factors influencing student-athlete graduation rates in higher education.* Boston University (1998)]. I went from being immersed in the slave narratives, Langston Hughes, Zora Neale Hurston, and Richard Wright from my Bachelor's and Master's programs straight to higher end thinking in multiple regressions. Like many doctoral students, I sought a statistics tutor and learned to establish the study, create the survey, set up the database, and run the analysis in StatView. My dissertation led to a multiple regression study published in one of the top higher education journals, *Journal of College Student Retention* [Hollis, *Journal of College Student Retention: Research, Theory & Practice, 3(3),* 265–284 (2001)]. After graduation, I then went on my merry way into administration, but still with a love for writing and research. During my administrative career, I had a great professional comrade in Dr. Earl Shaw, a renowned African American physicist at Rutgers-Newark. He was an African American gentleman who was raised in Mississippi and completed his doctorate at the University of California Berkeley; when he came to Rutgers-Newark, he brought a laser from Bell Labs. In his professional career in higher education, he discussed physics in a way that made so much sense to me. At the time, I was the director of the Learning Resource Center at Rutgers-Newark and knew that our students requested algebra tutoring more than tutoring on all other subjects combined. So I asked Dr. Shaw, "Why is it that our kids struggle with math?" His answer was an elegant one:

"When you are studying Ralph Ellison or even about Western Europe, it isn't foundational. You don't need to know Chaucer to get to Shakespeare to get to Mary Shelley to get to Phyllis Wheatly. In STEM, one must master each foundational step. Also, it requires concentration. Sure, you can put your headphones on and read *Frankenstein* on the subway. Close it when you get to your stop, and then reopen it. *Math?* You can't do that. You must have quiet and be undisturbed. Let's face it, our kids have so many distractions. If Mom is working a double, that student can't ignore his three little siblings. If a high school student has a job, then commuting, then housework, then biochemistry? Not happenin'. So many of our kids are trapped in their socio-economic position that even the smartest don't have extended and secure peace and quiet. So our kids struggle more in math and science. The approach to studying is different."

Dr. Shaw's answer always stuck with me. In short, he was saying those who come from compromised socio-economic backgrounds don't have that "room of their own" [Woolf, *A room of one's own and three guineas.* OUP Oxford (2015)] to study and analyze the wonders of math. I find that my brother, who is currently a stellar engineer, had quiet time and space, but we were blessed with our own rooms and our own desks and quiet time for homework (whether we liked it or not). But even in our own sleepy western Pennsylvania town, many students did not have such consistently quiet study environments. I kept this in mind through another ten years in student services.

When I switched my careers from administration to educational research, I still had predictive research questions, now about workplace bullying. For my first project, a colleague convinced me that with a researcher's training I should be clear that CITI standards are always followed. I created the instrument, tested it, and analyzed the data. The survey led to *Bully in the Ivory Tower* (2012), which still is a major success and the bedrock of my consulting. I then turned my focus to a tenure-track position and continued my survey research.

I say to the reader, remember, I am the English major, the one who loved Alice Walker and Gloria Naylor. My background embraced August Wilson, Ralph Wilson, and Nella Larson. Yet my questions led me to statistics. I read quite a bit and have taught Introduction to Quantitative Methods at a Research 2 Carnegie Classified institution for doctoral students. Even the prep for a statistics class is vastly different than a course relying on theoretical discussions.

Ten years later and with tenure, I have conquered math anxiety and found that young girl in me who went to algebra in her own red clogs. I could find myself in the data, and I have created a stable and uninterrupted space to learn statistics techniques. Now I tell my students if I—Leah, the English major who hated balancing a checkbook—could do it, you can too. Students who come from backgrounds that did not allow for sustained quiet space often dance around stats, even choosing qualitative methods for research before they have designed the study. This strategy often emerges in an attempt to avoid statistics. Many students state that they want qualitative research because the math scares them, or they just don't get it [Rodriguez, *Journal of Hispanic Higher Education, 13*(3), 191–205 (2014)]. If you're one of those students who came out of the humanities or arts, and now you want to ask your own social justice questions, this book is for you. Perhaps you're looking at a career in administration and policy development. Then statistics are needed to predict the best fiscal commitments. Even if one is not doing the calculations, one should be able to read the findings. From another vantage point, perhaps you are looking into social justice questions and want to develop your own data instead of searching for previously designed instruments and datasets.

Regardless of the reason, this book discusses the research questions and hypotheses for eight instruments. There will be a discussion on different ways to tackle the question. Each instrument has also been validated and will have an accompanying Cronbach's Alpha. New knowledge that leads to policy emerges from the numbers. The following chapters offer a pathway to minimize statistics anxiety for social justice solutions.

Keywords Workplace bullying • Instrument design • Qualitative data • Social justice

Introduction

Researchers and students often have empirical questions for which there is not an existing survey. Often researchers are told to find a survey that has already been validated. However, previously used instruments frequently do not always answer the questions posed for an innovative study. In the case of social justice issues, and, for me, specifically researching workplace bullying, I found that creating and validating my own instruments helps me create new scholarship instead of relying on past instruments. Researchers in emergent areas may also find the same problems. Survey research can collect data for statistical methods and qualitative methods. For example, I have created surveys that gather data via Likert scales for chi-square analyses and multiple regression, yet that same instrument can pose open-ended questions that collect data for qualitative content analysis and other methods that require coding.

LITERATURE REVIEW FIRST

A strength for the humanities and social science researcher should be the ability to glean theory and findings from previous studies before creating an instrument. For example, I initially used Professor Dennis Mithaug's equal opportunity theory (1996), which states that equal opportunity and access occur when barriers are removed. In my study of student athletes, I found the barrier to educational attainment was the actual athletic scholarship. Students are vying for starting time in their sport, while often missing class for practice, travel, games, or even athletic training appointments. In creating the instrument for the 1998 study, I kept obstacles in mind and sought to uncover which student athlete services truly helped student athletes transcend academic obstacles (Hollis, 1998).

For my more current research on workplace bullying, I read a great deal using Einarsen et al. (2003), Jurnak (2010), Keashly and Newman (2010), and Wiedmer (2010). Research before my first original instrument on workplace bullying confirmed that 37% of Americans face bullying at some time in their lifetimes (Namie & Namie, 2009). Hence I could work with a baseline percentage for those affected. Other authors, such as Djurkovic et al. (2008), Fritz (2014), and Lutgen-Sandvik and Arsht (2014), addressed productivity and turnover issues, inclusive of the cost. Given this reading, I generated instrument questions that asked participants about turnover intention and how employees managed day-to-day work life while trying to avoid a bully.

With each new study, I have returned to the literature to discover which new element can contribute to workplace bullying literature. For example, studies on workplace bullying and insomnia, PTSD, and anxiety helped me create questions for research on the relationship between workplace bullying and health problems (Conway et al., 2021; Nauman et al., 2019; Spence Laschinger & Nosko, 2015).

The ability to develop validated instrument questions is key to social justice research, especially regarding race and gender. Too often, empirical findings do not reflect race or intersectionality because communities of color are excluded from the sample. When I first began research on workplace bullying, there was negligible work on gender as a compelling factor. Hence, if a researcher can study Ackers's gendered organization (1990) or Fryed's organizational betrayal theories (2014), that researcher can craft questions that are disseminated, and which acquire data for statistical analysis. Also, to study Blacks, Latinx, Asians, and the LGBTQ community (Hollis & McCalla, 2013; Karenga, 2018), researchers often must over-sample these groups to obtain a sample large enough for a statistically valid analysis.

DEVELOPMENT AND DISSEMINATION

Typically, new researchers are advised to seek previously validated instruments to conduct their studies. This approach gives the researcher a convenient process by which to ask questions if, first, the researcher can find the appropriate instrument and second if the validated instrument serves to address the study questions. However, pre-existing instruments do not always provide a mechanism to gather new knowledge. I advocate that the researcher should be willing to create new questions and thereby create new findings. Instrument development requires several revisions through beta-testing to ensure the question language is clear. Therefore, once the researcher develops the questions, the instrument should be beta-tested with four to five experts who will give feedback about the language clarity and content. This process can be an opportunity to minimize the potential impact of researcher's bias as well (Dillman et al., 2014).

Once the instrument is developed, beta-tested, and tested for Cronbach's Alpha, which will be discussed later, the survey is ready for dissemination. The old school method was to send surveys via postal service. With a sample in which the researcher does not have email addresses, the postal service remains a viable option. The researcher should send an announcement post card to potential participants so that they can anticipate the study. For online studies, researchers can also send an announcement email alerting people to the upcoming study.

Fan and Yan (2010) stated that development includes consideration of delivery and completion. Hence, researchers should note that email systems typically do not allow distribution of large (over 500) emails for study. On the receiving end, such emails are considered spam. Additionally, commercial accounts such as Yahoo and AOL do not permit large distributions. The solution is to work with the IT department and ask them to create a safe list where all emails for the study are loaded into one name. For example, if I am studying community college coaches, I might call the safe list CCcoach@myschool.edu, and all the emails under that safe list will receive the invitation to participate. Such safe lists also are more successful at actual delivery to potential respondents, instead of being marked as spam or junk. For my research, I occasionally send an initial announcement, yet contrary to some researchers, I personally did not notice a difference in response rates. Nonetheless, introductions and announcements have merit. Edwards et al. (2002), Fox et al. (1988), and Yammarino et al. (1991) have commented that introductions with personalized messages may increase the response rate.

Similarly, researchers have various opinions regarding the announcement. Mail merge programs allow researchers to personalize the announcement and invitation. Nonetheless, Munoz-Leiva et al. (2009) argued that though personalization may motivate someone to answer questions, personalizing the announcements can make respondents wary that their answers will be personally identifiable. Research in controversial or provocative topics such as sex, abortion, gun violence, and corruption may make respondents hesitate to participate, and personalizing the announcement can further contribute to that hesitation (Platek, 1985). For online engagement, the researcher should send messages on Tuesday, Wednesday, or Thursday, at the height of the work week. Potential respondents are less likely to ignore weekday messages or overlook such messages if they take a long weekend.

The series for dissemination might seem insistent, but it works to achieve the desired sample. Please see Table 2.1.

Table 2.1 Sample dissemination schedule

Initial announcement
Postal service: Send bright-colored post card
Internet: Send brief email announcement
First round: Within seven days of announcement
Postal service: Send the survey in a bright envelope with a prepaid return envelope
Internet: Send brief invitation message with a link to the survey
Second round: Within 10–14 days of first round
Postal service: Send bright-colored post card as reminder
Internet: Announce it is the second round, thank those who completed, and send the link again. The reminder should occur on a Tuesday, Wednesday, or Thursday
Third round: Within 10–14 days of second round
Postal service: Send bright-colored post card as reminder
Internet: Announce it is the third round, thank those who completed, and send the link again. The reminder should occur on a Tuesday, Wednesday, or Thursday
Final round: Within 10–14 days of third round
Postal service: Send bright-colored post card as reminder
Internet: Announce it is the third round, thank those who completed, and send the link again. The reminder should occur on a Tuesday, Wednesday, or Thursday

If potential respondents do not answer within four reminders, researchers should assume they have opted out of the study. Further, in Internet dissemination, potential respondents may reply to have their names removed from the list. The researcher should remove the name immediately from future dissemination and confirm the person's request. The aforementioned dissemination schedule occurs over 50 days. Before launching the study, review the calendar so the data collection window does not fall over a long winter break or other anticipated interruption at work. For educational research, this means I should not launch studies that fall over commencement or the opening of an academic term. However, if one is conducting a study and purchasing the respondents through SurveyMonkey Audience, while the cost can be high, they have a very quick collection window in which the holidays and breaks do not seem to matter. Yet, note that collecting responses through SurveyMonkey Audience means only those who subscribe to SurveyMonkey reply. Those without regular computer access or the disposable income to have a SurveyMonkey account would not be approached through the SurveyMonkey™ Audience platform. To be blunt, in my experience, fewer people of color are on SurveyMonkey Audience and may not be accessible through the SurveyMonkey Audience option.

Note also that researchers coming from the humanities, arts and sciences might demystify this process by approaching instrument development as a creative process. The aesthetics of the instrument are important to engage potential respondents. SurveyMonkey™ offers. several templates, pictures, and colors available, but one should remember not to choose distracting, complex, or busy themes. Qualtrics is another popular survey platform.

In sample development and recruitment, respondents should remember the scope of their study. The Internet can reach large samples quickly, but this does not mean that all reachable participants will advance the study (Baatard, 2012). Researchers should use G*Power to determine the required sample size for their statistical study, with the goal of developing the *best* sample, not necessarily the largest sample. To this point, Baatard (2012) stated that one should avoid seeking "the largest number of respondents possible" if they do not serve the purposes of the study (p. 102). For example, I might want to study tutoring services at research institutions. If I find I do not have enough respondents in my sample, the solution is not to survey community college tutoring, unless I re-cast the central research question to examine higher education tutoring in all sectors, not just research institutions. In addition, the article's literature review and theory should then change in scope, too.

One solution is to change the central research question. For example, an original study might strive to investigate Chicanos in Wisconsin. However, the researcher might not be able to recruit enough Chicanos in Wisconsin, though the research could be groundbreaking. The solution might include expanding the sample to Hispanics, not just Chicanos (depending on the purpose of the study). The scope of the study could also be expanded to all states in the Central Time Zone, extending past the state of Wisconsin. These parameter changes from Chicano to Hispanic and from Wisconsin to all states in the Central Time Zone are viable modifications, but only if such modifications align with the purpose of the study.

BIAS MANAGEMENT

As researchers, we all have preconceived ideas about what we study. For example, I might posit that western Pennsylvania is flood prone, but the truth of the matter is I am from Johnstown, Pennsylvania, and lived through the 1977 flood. To state that Pennsylvania is a flood zone is to show my bias. If I ask questions, whether in qualitative or quantitative research, in a leading and presumptive manner, the bias remains and skews the research. When posing instrument questions, one should ask a question in a neutral manner.

I'll offer an example to clarify the point. I might design a survey on road rage that asks, "Do you always speed when you drive to work?" (Yes/no). In doing so, I am assuming that the respondent drives instead of taking public transportation. Instead, I could ask, "Could you describe your driving style on the way to work?" then offer Likert-scale options such as slow driver, neutral drive, fast driver, and breakneck driver, all listed in a logical order. Note, a possible answer should also include, "does not drive," because the question assumes the respondent drives at all. The respondent can give a more authentic answer than being led by the original prompt. I quote Krumpal (2013), who supported this vantage point: "Attempt to formulate and present questions in a neutral way to lower respondents' concerns about how the admission of a certain behavior will be judged. Researchers often write sensitive questions using unthreatening, euphemistic, familiar, and forgiving words or phrases" (p. 2036).

Using Demographics as a Filter

One of the best parts of data analysis is the multiple uses for the collected answers. Many of my instruments gather demographic data such as age range, gender, race, and job titles. One might have a research question such as "How many times are you told you must volunteer for service duties as part of your professor appointment?" The entire sample will answer. However, depending on how big the sample is, one can conduct a comparison, such as men compared to women. One can compare assistant professors to full professors. Additional questions can ask about the types of institutions (schools, hospitals, daycare) or ask for other demographic information such as rural, suburban, and urban. In my research, I am often comparing community colleges, four-year colleges and universities, minority-serving institutions, and historically Black colleges and universities. I also use demographics to analyze workplace bullying along racial and gender lines.

Elements to Consider in Instrument Design

Researchers often write an invitation introducing the study to potential respondents. I have learned from Dillman et al. (2014) to subordinate my position in announcements and invitations. Honestly, any study needs people to volunteer their five to seven minutes to advance research I remind my own students that people are not clamoring to answer their interview questions or survey questions. With this in mind, I definitely indicate in the recruitment letter to respondents that their insight is needed and appreciated. Further, when I focus on people of color, I clearly remark that little research is done on our population or their population of color. By answering the survey, they are contributing to authentic knowledge about that population.

Once respondents accept the invitation and access the survey, they should learn about the purpose of the study (dissertation, grant, primary research) and they should see the informed consent that explains risks, that makes it clear that their participation is voluntary. They may withdraw at any time, and that nothing will be personally identifiable. Further, the informed consent page should have the IRB # and the researcher's email to answer questions. Yes, people will write to ask questions about the survey. If a respondent does not agree to continue through the informed consent page, or opts not to proceed, the researcher should design the survey such that the respondent is automatically exited from the instrument.

Instrument development can also incorporate qualifying questions. For example, through SurveyMonkey Audience, I answered a survey that asked me if I liked a particular soda; I do not drink soda and answered accordingly. Then, I was immediately exited from the survey. A researcher might predetermine the sample by surveying only women in a study about women's issues, or a researcher might only survey army nurses, regardless of gender, if the study is about this group. One key element is to never guess participants' race, religion, age, gender, etc.; respondents should always self-identify such characteristics.

Aesthetics and Instrument Development

As respondents are often bombarded in their day-to-day world with email, spam, and phishing, they may not quickly engage a request to complete yet another instrument (Anseel et al., 2010). However, researchers can create messages and instruments that stand out in this digital flurry to increase response rates (Tourangeau et al., 2007). In addition to attractive colors and fonts, giving the instrument a brand, such as a home institution or foundation, lends more credibility to the instrument (Edwards et al., 2002). I have also found that potential respondents will Google the researcher. On more than one occasion, a potential respondent has written to me to state they checked me on Google Scholar and at my home institution to ensure that the study was legitimate.

Regardless of the survey platform, the aesthetics should be easy on the eye. For example, loud colors and neon colors challenge readability. Jewel tones and dark colors can oversaturate a computer monitor. Further, spacing and clear fonts are optimal; therefore, researchers should not cram questions onto a page. Joseph (2001) noted:

> Everything you do should be aimed at making the survey more interesting, attractive and easy to fill out and return. Any flaw in printing, poor choices of words or opening questions, anything that makes it take longer or be harder to fill out will ... result in smaller return rates. (p. 420)

For my SurveyMonkey instruments, I typically use Arial or Calibri because they are standard clean fonts that will not get mangled in browsers. Ornate and unique fonts may be interesting for the designer, but the end user may receive nonsense symbols when their smart phone or operating system cannot accommodate the fancy font. While minding the time, researchers should also take their own survey in several different browsers such as Google, Safari, and Firefox. Also, complete the survey on a smartphone and iPad, as many survey vendors have created platforms for those devices. Each time the researcher takes the survey, they should confirm the time required to complete the instrument. As noted previously, the survey should also be beta-tested, perhaps with a few friends, to check the time required for completion and get feedback on clear language and syntax (Orr, 2012).

QUESTIONING PARTICIPANTS

In writing questions, reflect on the audience who receives the questionnaire. Researchers should have IRB approval and therefore automatic protection for their respondents. However, even in an anonymous survey, people are reluctant to report sensitive and confidential information. With this in mind, researchers should be sure that the survey is in no way personally identifiable. For example, if one asks if someone is from an HBCU and then asks the state of the institution, in some cases, only two HBCUs are in one state, thereby making that respondent's answer not as anonymous, when one can figure out who replied. Another example might occur in a campus client survey. If the faculty development instrument asks for gender, of course people will choose male, female, fluid. Then another question in the survey might ask a specific discipline, and a woman from the classics department participates. If there is only one woman in the classics department, and she answered both questions truthfully, even though her name was not attached to the survey, her demographic responses personally identify her.

Also, note the time of year that a survey is launched. In my field of higher education, I conducted a survey of human resources professionals and gathered data in June and July before new faculty onboarding began. If I survey faculty, I do not launch a survey in the middle of drop/add periods or final exam periods.

QUESTION FORMATS

Instruments can present a variety of ways by which to engage participants. Multiple choice questions, Likert questions, rankings questions, and open-ended questions will be reviewed in this chapter. Instrument developers should note that potential respondents can become bored or annoyed, so the instrument should not ask random questions that do not advance the study or that confuse respondents. The invitations and reminders all should allude to the purpose of the study, hence questions that don't align with that purpose can affect the final sample (Moreno et al., 2006).

LIKERT-SCALE QUESTIONS

Dr. Rensis Likert created the Likert scale in 1931 while studying at Columbia University for his doctoral work (Likert, 1931). The scale is a symmetric approach to measuring attitudes and perceptions; the approach is used frequently in sociology, psychology, and other social science disciplines (Batterton & Hale, 2017; Croasmun & Ostrom, 2011). Subsequent researchers noted that the symmetry in the scale could be in three degrees (1 through 3), five degrees (1 through 5) or seven degrees (1 through 7), and found five degrees offer the most reliability (Croasmun & Ostrom, 2011; Guilford, 1954; Matell & Jacoby, 1971; Ray, 1980). An example of a Likert-style question is provided in Table 2.2.

OPEN ENDED QUESTIONS, A POWERFUL TOOL

Researchers typically use instrument studies when they have quantitative questions. However, the open-ended questions in surveys can allow researchers to engage in a mixed methods analysis. Data from open-ended remarks can be analyzed in a qualitative content analysis (Krippendorff, 2018) and used to triangulate the quantitative data. The open-ended

Table 2.2 Sample Likert-style question

	Don't agree	Neutral	Strongly agree	
Commuters have a tougher time in college	1	2 3 4	5	N/A[a]

[a]Be sure to include an "N/A" in case the respondent has no answer

comments can add another dimension to the quantitative data by garnering remarks about why or how a phenomenon occurred. Also, adding the option "other" in questions can bring in qualitative data ripe for analysis. Below are two sample questions designed to collect descriptive statistics and gather qualitative information through the open-ended option. I use two types of open-ended questions. One type includes the "other" option at the end of a specific question.

Example #1:

How did the flex time policy affect your health?

1. Less Stressful
2. Neutral
3. More Stressful
4. Other*_____

In this "other" option, respondents can remark on other information such as "the free time takes away structure" or "it gives me too much freedom." The "other" option gives respondents a method by which to offer their truth if the pre-determined options do not fit.

Example #2

How did the faculty respond to the training? (Check all that apply)

They found it engaging
They were not interested
They saw no application to their work
They saw it as a waste of time
Other: _____

In this "other" option, respondents can make more substantial comments about the training, such as the materials were dated, the trainer was rude, or training will help with students.

I also use open-ended questions as independent questions at the end of the instrument. After spending eight to ten minutes reflecting on a topic, the respondent has generated memories and reflections about the topic. By asking a final open-ended question, "What additional comments could you offer about [the topic]?" researchers can glean rich and unanticipated data. Through such questions for my workplace bullying research, respondents have reported extreme health problems, divorces, miscarriages, and suicidal ideation as part of their workplace bullying experiences. Therefore,

Table 2.3 Standalone open-ended question

Open-ended prompt: Are there any specific comments or insights you would like to share about workplace bullying in higher education?
Sample open-ended answers from respondents:
(A) It is an extremely horrible problem in higher education and there needs to be awareness programming and seminars. I also feel that confidential resources could help with workplace bullying.
(B) The norm being bullies running unchecked devouring the meek and weak in an organizational structure. The bullies pick on those that they believe they can bully but don't dare stand up against someone with on equal footing. It is sad to watch.

the open-ended questions give respondents an opportunity to share pertinent information in their own words. Often, these questions yield a robust dataset from which two or three themes emerge. Below is an example in Table 2.3.

MULTIPLE CHOICE QUESTIONS

As with many types of survey questions, multiple choice questions must be informed by the literature reviewed to create the research project. In workplace bullying research, I read that targeted employees will leave the organization (Goldblatt, 2007). Therefore, when investigating the impact on higher education employees, I can build on the literature. With the literature review, I could further consider how workplace bullying leads to self-isolation, anxiety, stress, and depression (Glasø & Notelaers, 2012; Hollis, 2016c; Lutgen-Sandvik & Arsht, 2014). Even when surveying a sample regarding proactive topics, the researchers should design questions that are not leading, negative, or complicated. Moreno et al. (2006) also stated that possible answers should be "autonomous, without overlapping or referring to other questions. For this reason, the options 'All of the above' or 'None of the above' should be avoided; and no option should stand out from the rest in either content or appearance" (p. 65). Overlapping options will only create problems for data analysis and confuse study participants.

ANALYSIS OF THE FOLLOWING EIGHT INSTRUMENTS

I see merit and validation in all types of research methods. Quantitative methods can measure and predict phenomena, while qualitative processes gather respondents' lived experiences and perceptions. Since quantitative data does not offer the rationale or backstory for the numbers, they can fail to provide the human depth in a problem.

For example, if one were to study community college students facing expulsion, quantitative methods can confirm the number of academic expulsions and even who was expelled. Qualitative methods, in contrast, can explore why students get expelled, such as discovering that commuting was too arduous, or unemployment affected student performance. In many ways, qualitative methods are considered a social justice approach because the voices of the disenfranchised are brought forward. Such voices are vitally important. However, qualitative studies tend to have very small samples when compared to quantitative research. With that in mind, if the researcher's goal is to better understand a phenomenon for a small sample, the qualitative process is appropriate. However, to set policy, I recommend quantitative approaches because using a larger sample makes the study more generalizable and applicable to a larger group.

*　*　*

The eight validated instruments in this book are available for public use, of course, with the proper citation. Each instrument will have the Cronbach's Alpha validation procedures, the findings, and publications that were a result. Releasing the instruments and guiding researchers through the validation process should inspire others to pursue social justice research with quantitative methods.

References

Anseel, F., Lievens, F., Schollaert, E., & Choragwicka, B. (2010). Response rates in organizational science, 1995–2008: A meta-analytic review and guidelines for survey researchers. *Journal of Business Psychology.*, *25*, 335–349. https://doi.org/10.1007/s10869-010-9157-6

Baatard, G. (2012). A technical guide to effective and accessible web surveys. *The Electronic Journal of Business Research Methods.*, *10*(2), 101–109. available online at www.ejbrm.com.

Batterton, K. A., & Hale, K. N. (2017). The Likert scale what it is and how to use it. *Phalanx, 50*(2), 32–39.

Conway, P. M., Høgh, A., Balducci, C., & Ebbesen, D. K. (2021). Workplace bullying and mental health. *Pathways of Job-Related Negative Behaviour*, 101–128.

Croasmun, J. T., & Ostrom, L. (2011). Using Likert-type scales in the social sciences. *Journal of Adult Education, 40*(1), 19–22.

Dillman, D. A., Smyth, J. D., & Christian, L. M. (2014). *Internet, phone, mail, and mixed-mode surveys: The tailored design method*. John Wiley & Sons.

Djurkovic, N., McCormack, D., & Casimir, G. (2008). Workplace bullying and intention to leave: The moderating effect of perceived organizational support. *Human Resource Management Journal, 18*(4), 405–422. https://doi.org/10.1111/j.1748-8583.2008.00081.x

Edwards, P., Roberts, I., Clarke, M., DiGuiseppi, C., Pratap, S., & Wentz, R. (2002). Increasing response rates to postal questionnaires: Systematic review. *BMJ, 324*, 1183.

Einarsen, S., Hoel, H., Zapf, D., Cooper, C. (Eds.) (2003). *Bullying and Emotional Abuse in the Workplace: International Perspectives in Research and Practice*. New York, NY: Taylor & Francis.

Fan, W., & Yan, Z. (2010). Affecting response rates of the web survey: A systemic review. *Computers in Human Behavior., 26*, 132–139.

Fox, R. J., Crask, M. R., & Kim, J. (1988). Mail survey response rate: A meta-analysis of selected techniques for inducing response. *Public Opinion Quarterly, 52*, 467–491.

Fritz, J. (2014). Organizational misbehavior. In J. C. Lipinski & M. Laura (Eds.), *Bullying in the workplace: Causes symptoms, and remedies* (pp. 3–16). Routledge.

Glasø, L., & Notelaers, G. (2012). Workplace bullying, emotions, and outcomes. *Violence and Victims, 27*(3), 360–377.

Goldblatt, V. (2007). Bye-bye bullies: How to get people to want to work: Conflict, fault-finding and rights-based hierarchical structures are unproductive. Such tedious bully tactics no longer cut it. *New Zealand Management, 54*(4), 39–41. From ABI/INFORM Global (Document ID: 1291917771).

Guilford, J. P. (1954). *Psychometric methods*. McGraw-Hill.

Hollis, L. P. (2016). Bruising the bottom line: Cost of workplace bullying and the compromised access for underrepresented community college employees. In *The Coercive Community College: Bullying and its costly impact on the mission to serve underrepresented populations* (pp. 1–26). Emerald Group Publishing Limited.

Hollis, L. P. (2016a). Cybershaming–technology, cyberbullying, and the application to people of color. In *The Coercive Community College: Bullying and its costly impact on the mission to serve underrepresented populations* (pp. 125–135). Emerald Group Publishing Limited.

Hollis, L. P. (2016b). The importance of professor civility in a computer-based open-access environment for a minority-serving institution. In *The Coercive Community College: Bullying and its costly impact on the mission to serve underrepresented populations* (pp. 65–82). Emerald Group Publishing Limited.

Hollis, L. P. (2016c). Socially dominated: The racialized and gendered positionality of those precluded from bullying. In *The Coercive Community College: Bullying and its costly impact on the mission to serve underrepresented populations* (pp. 103–112). Emerald Group Publishing Limited.

Hollis, L. P. (1998). *Equal opportunity for student-athletes: Factors influencing student-athlete graduation rates in higher education.* Boston University.

Hollis, L. P. (2001). Service ace? Which academic services and resources truly benefit student athletes. *Journal of College Student Retention: Research, Theory & Practice, 3*(3), 265–284.

Hollis, L. P., & McCalla, S. A. (2013). Bullied back in the closet. *Journal of Psychological Issues in Organizational Culture, 4*(2), 6–16.

Joseph, J. (2001). Survey research design. *Library Hi Tech, 19*(4), 419–421.

Jurnak, M. (2010). The cost of losing good employees. *New Hampshire Business Review, 32*(1), 21.

Karenga, M. (2018). Founding the First PhD in Black Studies: A Sankofa Remembrance and Critical Assessment of Its Significance. *Journal of Black Studies, 49*(6), 576–603.

Keashly, L., & Neuman, J. H. (2010). Faculty experiences with bullying in higher education: Causes, consequences, and management. *Administrative Theory & Praxis, 32*(1), 48–70.

Krippendorff, K. (2018). *Content analysis: An introduction to its methodology.* Sage publications.

Krumpal, I. (2013). Determinants of social desirability bias in sensitive surveys. *A Literature Review. Quality and Quantity, 47*(4), 2025–2047.

Likert, R. (1931). A technique for the measurement of attitudes. *Archives of Psychology, 22*(140), 1–55.

Lutgen-Sandvik, A., & Arsht, S. (2014). How unaddressed bullying affects employees, workgroups, workforces, and organizations: The widespread aversive effects of toxic communication climates. In J. C. Lipinski & M. Laura (Eds.), *Bullying in the workplace: Causes, symptoms, and remedies* (pp. 51–68). Routledge.

Mardon, A., Singh, J., Schuler, M., Bilal, H., Jean-Marie, N., George, M. E., et al. (2021). *The Nazca lines.* Golden Meteorite Press.

Matell, M. S., & Jacoby, J. (1971). Is there an optimal number of alternatives for Likert scale items? Study I: Reliability and validity. *Educational and Psychological Measurement, 31*(3), 657–674.

Mithaug, D. E. (1996). *Equal opportunity theory: Fairness in liberty for all.* Sage Publications.

Moreno, R., Martínez, R. J., & Muñiz, J. (2006). New guidelines for developing multiple-choice items. Methodology. *European Journal of Research Methods for the Behavioral and Social Sciences, 2*(2), 65–72.

Munoz-Leiva, F., Sanchez-Fernandez, J., Montoro-Rios, F., & Ibanez-Zapata, J. (2009). Improving the response rate and quality in web-based survey through personalization and frequency of reminder mailing. *Quality and Quantity, 44,* 1037–1052. https://doi.org/10.1007/s11135-009-9256-5

Namie, G., & Namie, R. (2009). *The bully at work: What you can do to stop the hurt and reclaim your dignity on the job.* Sourcebooks.

Nauman, S., Malik, S. Z., & Jalil, F. (2019). How workplace bullying jeopardizes employees' life satisfaction: The roles of job anxiety and insomnia. *Frontiers in Psychology, 10,* 2292.

Orr, L. (2012). The rise of the smart phone: Are you leveraging mobile? 10 tips for mobile friendly survey creation. *Alert, 52*(3), 32–34.

Platek, R. (1985). Some important issues in questionnaire development. *Journal of Official Statistics, 1*(2), 119–136.

Ray, J. (1980). How many answer categories should attitude and personality scales use? *South African Journal of Psychology, 10,* 53–54.

Rodriguez, B. A. (2014). The threat of living up to expectations: Analyzing the performance of Hispanic students on standardized exams. *Journal of Hispanic Higher Education, 13*(3), 191–205.

Spence Laschinger, H. K., & Nosko, A. (2015). Exposure to workplace bullying and post-traumatic stress disorder symptomology: The role of protective psychological resources. *Journal of Nursing Management, 23*(2), 252–262.

Tourangeau, R., Couper, M. P., & Conrad, F. (2007). Color, labels, and interpretive heuristics for response scales. *Public Opinion Quarterly, 71*(1), 91–112.

Wiedmer, T. (2010). Workplace bullying: Costly and preventable. *Delta Kappa Gamma Bulletin, 77*(2), 35–41.

Woolf, V. (2015). *A room of one's own and three guineas.* OUP Oxford.

Yammarino, F. J., Skinner, S. J., & Childers, T. L. (1991). Understanding mail survey response behavior. *Public Opinion Quarterly, 55,* 613–629.

CHAPTER 3

Bully in the Ivory Tower: A Baseline Study Validating Workplace Bullying in American Higher Education (2012)

Abstract Although the Scandinavians had been studying workplace bullying in all sectors for decades, previous researchers had not started an in-depth look at workplace bullying in American higher education as of 2012. A few salient research articles were in existence at the time. My first study was designed to begin filling this gap. Hence, this chapter will review the rationale and process for the *Bully in the Ivory Tower* study [Hollis, *Bully in the ivory tower: How aggression & incivility erode American higher education*. Patricia Berkly LLC (2012)]. This research was my baseline study for workplace bullying in American higher education. Additionally, "Bully University," which I published with Sage in 2015, emerged from these findings and was the initial cost analysis of workplace bullying. Theoretically, *Bully in the Ivory Tower* uses Arlie Hochschild's [*American Journal of Sociology, 85*(3), 551–575 (1979)] emotional labor theory because it is exhausting to maintain composure while a bully thrashes one's calm. The "Bully University" article uses employee disengagement theories to explain why employee disengagement is more costly than employee turnover [Byrne, *Understanding employee engagement: Theory, research and practice*. Routledge (2015)]. The results of that study with Sage confirmed that 62% of respondents had been affected by workplace bullying within 18 months of the study. Further, bullied colleagues spend an average of 3.9 hours weekly, or five weeks annually, coping with and strategizing around bullies. The study, which relied on descriptive statistics and qualitative data, resulted in four peer-reviewed articles.

© The Author(s), under exclusive license to Springer Nature Switzerland AG 2024
L. P. Hollis, *Instrumental Social Justice in Higher Education*,
https://doi.org/10.1007/978-3-031-49289-1_3

Keywords Survey development • Workplace bullying • Descriptive
statistics

MOTIVATION FOR THE BASELINE STUDY

Before this study, I researched student athletes as an at-risk population.
Further, since African American student athletes in revenue sports tended
to have the lowest graduation rates, I was already tuned into race issues as
a research topic in higher education. Further, my background in African
American literature gave me insight into social justice issues. I had published a book about filing a complaint with the EEOC and had delivered
several trainings to human resources personnel nationwide about protected class and Title VII. I used Mithaug's (1996) *Equal Opportunity
Theory*, which states that for people to advance through opportunity,
obstacles to success should be removed.

In my administrative career, I led several trainings about diversity and
access. I worked with various universities to assist with learning disability
services. Even as an administrator, I was known for my commitment to
diversity. In this vein, a colleague asked me, "Does one have to be in a
protected class (race, gender, age, religion, color, ethnicity, disability, and
so forth) to avoid harassment at work?" My immediate thought was that
everyone should have a safe workspace. I then launched myself into the
literature to read about workplace bullying in higher education.

At the time in 2011, there was precious little on the topic except for a
great article by Keashly and Neuman (2010) about faculty bullying. Twale
and De Luca (2008) had penned a book about faculty incivility in 2008. I
was also aware of an emerging anthology about workplace bullying in
higher education. In my first workplace bullying study, I relied on Namie
and Namie's (2009) *The Bully at Work*, which was largely based on descriptive statistics; their book confirmed that 37% of American employees experienced workplace bullying some time in their careers. Consequently,
workplace bullying was deemed a silent epidemic, with over a third of the
population affected.

Because the Scandinavians have been the leaders in workplace research,
I relied on their definition for workplace bullying as I developed the study
and included the definition in the instrument (Einarsen et al., 2011). In
later studies, I presented their definition and asked respondents to apply it
to their higher education experiences. Therefore, with my belief that
higher education was populated by enlightened people who cared about
students and each other, I was beyond shocked that 62% of employees in

higher education were affected by workplace bullying (Hollis, 2012). Two of three people in higher education reported being affected by workplace bullying. Some potential respondents wrote to me asking why I limited the window to 18 months. If I had asked if they were bullied three years ago, they would reply affirmatively. In fact, I tabulated the numbers three times and was stunned at the results. Since this time, studies with other samples have resulted in the same findings, with 58% to 64% of respondents reporting that they have been affected by workplace bullying and that their respective universities seem not to care.

In the early 2000s, bullying was seen primarily as a grade school issue. Olweus (1994) stated the Scandinavians led bullying research, with other countries such as Japan, England, and Australia also addressing school-level bullying. Some argued that victims had a certain profile, inclusive of low self-esteem (Smith et al., 2001). Swearer et al. (2010) joined other researchers who linked bullying to adjustment problems, relationship problems, anxiety, depression, and academic performance issues (Batsche & Knoff, 1994; Graham et al., 2003; Hawker & Boulton, 2000; Nansel et al., 2003). The most disconcerting finding from the research was the link between school bullying and suicide (Kaltiala-Heino et al., 1999).

In 1999, bullied assailants from Columbine High School killed ten students and a teacher, then turned the guns on themselves (Muschert & Peguero, 2010). Since that time, many states have seen that bullying leads to violence, and they have passed anti-bullying laws for the K-12 level. All 50 states have some type of anti-bullying legislation, with Montana being the last state to pass legislation in 2015 (Ladika, 2018). Understandably, many studies examine the details that contributed to the rash of school shootings; however, workplace violence and aggression in higher education did not receive the same attention.

Design and Methods

Unlike later workplace bullying studies that I conducted, I designed this initial study for a baseline examination. In 2012, the literature had not considered the frequency of workplace bullying, who might be the bully, or what workplace bullying cost organizations in the higher education context. Also, I did not establish variables for multiple regression or other advanced statistical analyses for this baseline study. However, I could use the data from this data intake for two other studies that focused on young people under 35 and on women (Hollis, 2014, 2015b). When I filtered the data by race, I could also present findings specific to African American respondents.

Decision on Sample/Population

To recruit the sample, I collected 18 names from the publicly available websites of 175 four-year, baccalaureate-granting colleges and universities: two from alumni affairs/development, two from arts and letters faculty, two from science faculty, two from human resources, two from student affairs, two from admissions, two from athletics, two from information technology, and two from the executive level. Compiling this sample resulted in 3150 emailed invitations to complete the study. My career to that point had primarily been in administration; ergo, I was interested in administrative experience. I also wanted to collect responses from administrators across the university setting. Gradually, my work shifted to researching the faculty experience.

DISSEMINATION CYCLE IN 2012

From my doctoral work, I understood that for potential respondents to complete the study, they should get an invitation and then three reminders to complete the study. When I utilized this process, the most considerable boost to participation came in the second reminder. In contrast with my doctoral work 15 years previously, instead of using paper surveys sent through the postal service, I could use SurveyMonkey in 2012 and send the link via email to recruit respondents from 22 states on the East Coast.

Since I was new to survey distribution via the Internet, I learned the hard way that I could not send close to 3000 emails through AOL, MSN, or Yahoo. The ".com" designation resulted in emailed invitations being blocked by MSN, or the various firewalls at colleges and universities led to invitations being undeliverable. Therefore, in early 2012 when I collected the data, I used a mail merge service and the server at the local library, which was more acceptable to educational systems. Specifically, I chose the SendBlaster™ software, which allowed me to send mass emails more likely to bypass college and university firewalls. Despite my efforts, over 450 emails were undeliverable. Since 2012, I have learned to ask my home institution's IT department to create a safe list of all emails. This means that instead of a series of single emails being sent at once and then being flagged as spam, most emails are part of a safe list. The Gmail-based safe list enables me to send bulk emails without those invitations being caught in firewalls.

CRONBACH'S ALPHA FOR INSTRUMENT

When writing a grant proposal or submitting a paper to a high-end journal, reviewers want to confirm that the data in the study are valid. Since the findings are directly related to the instrument's validity, researchers should take care to tabulate the level of internal consistency for the survey by employing Cronbach's Alpha (Oncu et al., 2015). This is because Cronbach's Alpha evaluates if the scales in the instrument are closely related. Instruments with stronger statistical power yield more reliable and valid findings.

According to Cronbach (1951), a researcher can use an alpha coefficient method to validate Likert-scale questions; further, Oncu et al. (2015) confirmed that the Cronbach's Alpha process is appropriate for true-false questions. Therefore, assigning Likert-scales values to multiple choice questions and evaluating questions for yes/no outcomes was the process I used for applying Cronbach's Alpha to this instrument.

My validating the instrument included conducting a Cronbach's Alpha tabulation with Excel. Instrument analysis resulting in a Cronbach's Alpha at 0.65 or above is considered sufficient, as 0.65 rounds up to the required 0.7 for acceptable reliability (Bujang et al., 2018). A Cronbach's Alpha at 0.64 or below is not acceptable; if the Cronbach's Alpha coefficient is too low, this means the instrument is not valid and will not result in reliable findings.

For example, an instrument with a Cronbach's Alpha of 0.47 would be very weak, and the resulting data would not be reliable. Conversely, an instrument that produced a Cronbach's Alpha of 0.88 would have strong validity and the resulting data would be considered reliable. In short, the closer the relationship among instrument questions, the stronger the instrument is as a whole. The closer to 1.0 the Cronbach's Alpha variable is, the more reliable the instrument. The goal of the Cronbach's Alpha is to confirm that the instrument's results are valid and reliable. I used the following steps:

Step 1: Conduct a pilot test to gather 50 complete responses for the Cronbach's Alpha analysis. Researchers have noted a sample of 10 to 40 is required to conduct the Cronbach's Alpha (Bonett, 2002; Fleiss, 1986; Hertzog, 2008). However, other researchers have commented that the Cronbach calculation is stronger when more or all responses are included

(Ercan et al., 2007). Therefore, I relied upon answers from 50 respondents. Create an Excel spreadsheet with the questions, labeling the top columns and the respondents' answers in the rows. Be sure to have the data analysis tool pack included in Excel.

Step 2: For each completed respondent, insert the numeral answer for each question. In this instrument, 18 questions were analyzed. See Fig. 3.1 for how to create and populate the spreadsheet. The instrument's first ten questions included the informed consent and collected demographic information such as gender, race, sexual orientation, and salary. Figure 3.1 only shows the Excel sheet for questions 10 through 17, but all 50 respondents' answers are put into the spreadsheet.

Step 3: Calculate the variance in each question using the variance function: = VAR.S(B2:B21).

When question 10 (column B) is analyzed, the variance = 0.259607843. Similarly, when question 11 (column C) is analyzed, the variance = 0.17254902. This function should be applied to all columns resulting in a variance answer for each. For this instrument, 18 variances were

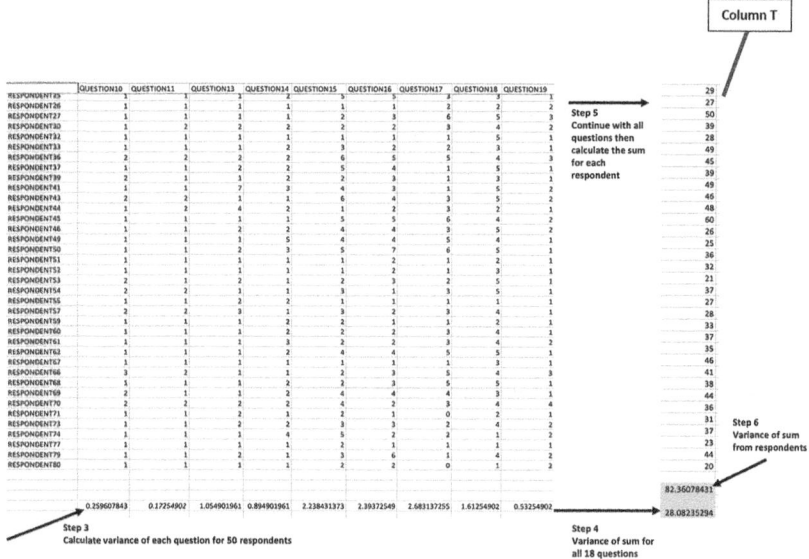

Fig. 3.1   Creating Excel sheet for Cronbach's Alpha analysis

tabulated for each of the questions. See Fig. 3.1 for steps three through six to conduct a Cronbach's Alpha.

Step 4: Once the variance for each column is tabulated, the sum of variance should be tabulated = SUM(B56:T56). The sum of variance for all 18 columns = 28.08235294. This is Σs^2_i.

Step 5: Tabulate the sum total for each respondent row. For example, the sum for questions 10, 11, and 13 through 33 for Respondent 80 equals 20. Note that I dropped question 12 from the analysis so it is not included in the Cronbach's Alpha tabulation. The sum for Respondent 79 equals 44. Note, for example, Respondent 78 was skipped because the individual did not complete the survey.

Step 6: There should now be a final column for the sum of each respondent. Next, use the sum variance function to analyze the final sum column = VAR.S(T2:T52) with the resulting variable equaling 82.36078431. This is $s^2 y$.

Step 7: The Cronbach's Alpha formula is:

$$\alpha = \frac{(n)}{(n-1)} * \frac{\left(s^2_y - \Sigma s^2_i\right)}{\left(s^2_y\right)}$$

N = the number of questions = 18
Therefore, for the *Bully in the Ivory Tower* instrument:

$$\alpha = \left(\frac{(18)}{(17)}\right) * \frac{\left(82.36\{\text{variance of sum column}\} - 28.08\{\text{sum of variance}\}\right)}{\left(82.36\{\text{variance of sum column}\}\right)}$$

The Cronbach's Alpha for the *Bully in the Ivory Tower* instrument = 0.698, rounded to 0.70.

* * *

REFLECTION

When I reflect on this first workplace bullying instrument from over 12 years ago, I think of what I would change. For this first instrument, I did not include the definition for workplace bullying; nonetheless, the definition influenced my thinking during survey development. However, in later studies, I explicitly offered a definition from Einarsen et al. (2011), or I used the Short Negative Acts Questionnaire (Notelaers et al., 2019). Over the past ten years, our society has been more receptive to gender-fluid people; hence, later instruments provided a gender-fluid or transgender option.

I also eliminated a question:
Are you afraid for your job if you speak up to defend against bullying?
Yes, I am concerned and would not speak up.
No, I would defend myself or another from a bully.

Once I collected the data and re-read the question, which had been beta-tested, I realized the wording was not clear. Did I mean "YES," the respondent is afraid for their job, and therefore, would not speak up? Perhaps "NO" means the respondent is not afraid for their job and would speak up. I was not confident with this question and how participants interpreted it. In retrospect, I realized this was a compound question. I could not determine if the responders were answering because they agreed with one part of the question or both parts. I had no choice but to eliminate the question from any data analysis. Said another way, the question was not valid, and the resulting data were not valid either. Even with beta-testing by other colleagues, this is an example of how a researcher might have to eliminate a question during analysis and reword it for a future study.

POWER OF OPEN-ENDED QUESTIONS

Once the quantitative data were collected, I had several open-ended remarks that inspired me to interview higher education colleagues. While a level of 62% of respondents reporting bullying was shocking for me at the time, other comments from respondents highlighted their concerns about why or how bullying eroded their work life. After examining the open-ended remarks, I interviewed nine higher education administrators for 60–75 minutes. These interviews yielded five themes and gave depth to the descriptive statistics in the quantitative portion.

1. Theme #1 Leadership drives organizational culture. All nine participants noted that the leader sets the tone for the educational environment. If a leader is kind and empathetic, employees adopt such behaviors. However, if a leader did not support policy and acted like a tyrant, the environment would be toxic. Quotes from the partici-

pants included "I feel like a DISPOSABLE employee" and also "…sure, it is tough for women to rise in the ranks. But the woman does not have to be a tyrant." Another respondent stated, "The bully willingly and knowingly manipulated and forced decisions that federal regulations did not support."

2. Theme #2 The cost of bad behavior. This second theme inspired the "Bully University" article about cost analysis. Respondents commented on how a disruptive bully in the executive office destroyed an afternoon of work. A vice president would become enraged and hurl a stapler across his office every two to three weeks. When he did such, the office was stifled. Over six years of ignoring this vice president's abhorrent behavior, the small college lost over $65,000 in wasted time dodging hurled staplers and avoiding this man's tantrums. Another respondent witnessed bullying in an athletic department. Two women filed lawsuits, and the development office could not raise money given those lawsuits. In reflection, this respondent noted that over $10 million was lost in legal fees, payouts, disengagement, and NCAA violations.

3. Theme #3 Coping with the bully's tactics. Regarding coping, one colleague commented, "I am too young to lose my hair like this." Her reaction to a toxic culture full of bullies was to stay locked in her office to avoid aggressive faculty who were constantly yelling and cursing at her over a student service schedule. The vice president knew about the deplorable behavior in this environment but did nothing. Other participants noted that they relied on spirituality and a belief in a divine power to cope with the abuse. A common coping mechanism was isolating oneself from office life. Employees remained in their offices with closed doors and faces planted behind a computer screen to avoid the executive bully. The situation was so bad that they would email each other rather than walk across the hall to ask a question.

4. Theme #4 The role of human resources. One recurring issue in the workplace bullying literature is that human resources departments worsen the situation. Respondents noted the boss didn't know about federal law or didn't care. Many stated that human resources departments were more interested in ignoring the mess than fixing it. Overall, respondents thought human resources was ineffective in dealing with workplace bullying. This theme inspired my book on human resource perspectives (Hollis, 2021).

5. Theme #5 Impact on student services. Respondents noted that they worked extra hard to serve students even though they themselves were abused on the job. Helping others seemed to temporarily assuage the perception of bullying. Though respondents' dedication to students kept them serving students, they also commented that a school fighting itself could not provide the best service for students.

*   *   *

I share these themes because the interview protocol emerged from the open-ended remarks reported in the survey. The findings reported in the descriptive statistics had established a new benchmark for bullying in higher education. However, I found it critical to understand why these problems existed. For researchers developing such instruments, the use of open-ended questions to inform a later interview protocol often yields a robust study that better explains why the phenomena are occurring.

The resulting publications:

Hollis, L. P. (2012). *Bully in the ivory tower: How aggression & incivility erode American higher education.* Patricia Berkly LLC, Wilmington DE.

Bully in the Ivory Tower study was the baseline inaugural study about workplace bullying in higher education. I gathered data from 401 participants at four-year colleges and universities. I chose 18 administrators from each school. The salient findings were that 62% of respondents reported facing bullying within the 18 months preceding the study. Data also confirmed that the leadership was the architect of the environment. If the leaders admonished bullies, then that abusive behavior did not occur. However, when the leader was a bully or ignored bullying, the aggressive behaviors continued. The finding about leadership remains consistent through workplace bullying research about any setting.

Hollis, L. P. (2015). Bully university? The cost of workplace bullying and employee disengagement in American higher education. *Sage Open, 5*(2), 2158244015589997.

Published in Sage Open, "Bully University" was a cost analysis of workplace bullying. By collecting the respondents' salaries and determining their hourly rate, I could calculate the cost through analyzing the time lost, ruminating, and strategizing about bullying per salary band. To date, this article is the most cited by fellow researchers.

Hollis, L. P. (2014). Lambs to slaughter? Young people as the prospective target of workplace bullying in higher education. *Journal of Education and Human Development, 3*(4), 45–57.

By using the age filter, I examined the departure trends of younger employees. Those 35 and younger will stay in a toxic environment for about two to three years. Then they depart, often taking organizational memory with them.

Hollis, L. P. (2015a). Take the bull by the horns: Structural approach to minimize workplace bullying for women in American higher education. Oxford Forum on Public, 2015(1), 1–13.

The instrument questions asked how respondents reacted to bullying. By analyzing the respondents' gender in this context, I confirmed that women are more likely to engage the organizational structures via formal complaints to human resources and supervisors. This trend aligns with women's previous workplace resistance against sexual harassment. This paper was also presented at the Oxford Roundtable, Oxford University.

RESULTING CONFERENCES

After the 2012 publication, I quickly learned that workplace bullying is an international topic with a host of international researchers. As a result, I have presented workplace bullying research in England, France, Saudi Arabia, Italy, Greece, New Zealand, Cuba, the Czech Republic, and Canada.

Cost of Workplace Bullying in American Higher Education. 9th International Congress on Workplace Bullying and Harassment. University of Milan, Milan, Italy. (2014)

By collecting salaries and the time respondents spent strategizing about workplace bullying, I could identify the cost per person. This data set returned a finding that 3.9 hours per week are spent on average per person. This leads to five weeks a year lost to workplace bullying. The findings were well received at this conference and a precursor to the article "Bully University."

That Old Black Magic: How Workplace Bullying Affects African American Creativity. 2nd National Conference of Black Doctoral Network, Philadelphia, Pennsylvania. (2014)

I had previously studied creativity and the environments which yield innovation. A mind at ease is creative, while a stressed mind must be concerned with safety and survival. As a result, I could filter the findings and then use applied creativity theory to examine how African American respondents were distracted dealing with a bully instead of creating solutions on the job.

Black on Black Crime: Intra-cultural Struggles and Bullying in the Workplace. 1st National Conference of Black Doctoral Network Philadelphia, Pennsylvania. (2013)

Einarsen et al.'s (2011) rules of bullying do not protect employees under Title VII. This means a white male can bully a fellow white male, leaving the target with little recourse because there is no race or gender difference.

REFLECTIVE QUESTIONS

The book and its chapters are meant to help new and seasoned researchers conduct Cronbach's Alpha for original instruments. Further, the instruments in this book can be used for research; of course, be sure to give the proper citation if one or any of the questions are used or modified for future research. The reflective questions in each chapter are meant to assist instructors in teaching Cronbach's Alpha processes.

1. This chapter reflects on a data collection process that had a specific focus, workplace bullying. The study was in a relatively new area when launched in 2012. As you consider your study, what compelling elements must you consider so you can recruit a proper sample?
2. To conduct this study specifically in higher education, I needed to gather emails from public websites. Consider the population you might want to study. How can you get access to them so you can conduct your study?
3. What is the most difficult part of the Cronbach's Alpha process for you? Please identify the issue to discuss with your professor/ instructor.
4. This instrument supported a full-length book, *Bully in the Ivory Tower*. How can you develop an instrument that also produces robust data for longer publications?
5. How could you re-cast this instrument to conduct a multiple regression or chi-square? How would you change the questions to collect data appropriate for such an analysis?

APPENDIX: THE INSTRUMENT

Bully in the Ivory Tower *(2012)*

Demographic Questions Not Part of Cronbach Alpha Calculation
Please check your age range:

18–23
24–28
29–35
36–40
41–49
50–60
61+

Are you White, Black or African American, American Indian or Alaskan Native, Asian, Native Hawaiian or other Pacific islander, or some other race?

White
Black or African American
Hispanic/Latino
American Indian or Alaskan Native
Asian
Native Hawaiian or other Pacific Islander
From multiple
Other
What is your gender?
Male
Female
What is your sexual orientation?
Straight/heterosexual
Gay/Lesbian
Bisexual
What is your income range at your institution?
$15,000–$25,000
$25,001–$35,000
$35,001–$45,000
$45,001–$55,000
$55,001–$65,000
$65,001–$75,000
$75,001–$85,000

$85,001–$95,000
$95,001–$105,000
$105,001–$125,000
$125,001–$150,000
Over $150,001
What is the highest educational level that you completed?
Two-year degree
Bachelor's
Master's
Doctorate
What is your religion?
Protestant
Catholic
Jewish
Hinduism
Muslim
Buddhist
Spiritual (no specific religion)
Atheist
Other (please specify)
Following questions
Which set of titles best reflect your current position in higher education?
Counselor/Advisor
Assist Director, Coordinator
Manager Director
Assistant/Associate Dean
Dean/Department Chair
Assistant Professor (non-tenured)
Associate or Full Professor (tenured)
Assistant/Associate Vice President/Vice Provost
Executive Director
Provost/Vice President
President
Other (please specify)
In regard to bullying in the academy… (check all that apply)
I have been bullied within the last 18 months.
I have witnessed bullying in the last 18 months.
I have NOT witnessed or experienced bullying in the last 18 months.
I have intentionally intimidated and bullied others.

In regard to VICARIOUS bullying (boss sends assistant or other staff to do his/her bullying) in the academy... (check all that apply)

I have been VICARIOUSLY bullied in the last 18 months.

I have witnessed VICARIOUS bullying in the last 18 months.

I have NOT witnessed or experienced VICARIOUS bullying in the last 18 months.

I have intentionally used a subordinate staff member to intimidate and bully others.

In your experience, what is the EDUCATIONAL level of the TARGET? Your experience means happened to you OR you witnessed it. (Check up to two options)

High school diploma or equivalent

Associates or 2-year degree

Bachelor's degree

Master's degree

Doctorate degree

Everyone can be a bully.

I have not witnessed bullying.

In your experience, what is the ORGANIZATIONAL level of the TARGET? Your experience means happened to you OR you witnessed it. (May check two options)

Entry Level/Administrative Support Assistant Director

Director

Non-tenured faculty Tenured Faculty

Assistant or Associate Dean

Assistant or Associate Vice President/Provost Vice President or Provost President

I have not witnessed or experienced bullying

Other

(Please specify)

Where were the TARGETS bullied? (Check all that apply)

Individual (one-on-one) meeting in front of students

In front of other staff

In cyberspace (email, chat room, bulletin board, etc.)

In local staff meeting

In division wide or department wide meeting

Other (please specify)

In regard to communication, how are TARGETS bullied? (Check all that apply)

Verbally endured insults and yelling

Verbally endured inappropriate jokes and teasing

Subject to group gossip and rumors

Face threats of job loss/being fired

Ignored, overlooked

Written embarrassment (harsh memos, notes or commands)

Other (please specify)

In regard to organizational expectations, how were TARGETS bullied? (Check all that apply)

Assigned unreasonable deadlines.

Excluded from lunches or other social office gatherings. Assigned unreasonable tasks.

Must comply with unreasonable accountability and reporting (minute by minute updates).

Their goals or tasks were changed abruptly without notice.

Their responsibilities, budget or reporting structure were abruptly changed without notice.

Other (please specify)

How long did the TARGET endure bullying?

One academic term

Two academic terms

Full calendar year

2–3 calendar years

More than 3 calendar years

Which strategies provided relief for the TARGET (whether yourself or someone you witnessed as a target)? (Check up to three options)

Report to supervisors

Report to HR

Leave department

Take more sick time Isolate self from group

There was no relief

Other (please specify)

How did the TARGET react to being bullied? (Check up to three options)

Report to supervisors

Report to HR

Leave department (transferred internally)

Take more sick time

Isolate self from group Resigned/Quit

Other (please specify)

If you are the target of bullying or witnessed bullying, approximately how much time does the target spend strategizing on ways to AVOID the bully?

One hour a week

Two hours a week

Three hours a week

Four hours a week

Five hours a week

Six hours a week

A full day total over a week

I have not endured or witnessed bullying

If bullying occurs in your department or division, how many people have left (or were separated from) the institution in the last 18 months to AVOID the toxic environment?

0

1

2

3

4

5

6

More than 6

In your experience, what is the EDUCATIONAL level of the BULLY? Your experience means happened to you OR you witnessed it. (May check two options)

Associates or 2-year degree

Bachelor's degree

Master's degree

Doctorate degree

Everyone can be a bully

In your experience, what is the ORGANIZATIONAL level of the BULLY? Your experience means happened to you OR you witnessed it. (May check two options)

Entry Level/Admin support

Assistant Director

Non-tenured faculty Tenured faculty

Assistant/Associate Dean

Assistant or Associate Vice President/Provost

Vice President or Provost
President
How did the organization deal with the BULLY? (Check up to three options)
Did nothing
Coached the BULLY
Fired the TARGET
Transferred BULLY to another department
Supported the BULLY
Transferred TARGET to another department
Fired the BULLY
If you work in or manage a work environment with a bully, how does the recession affect you? (Choose all that apply)
I tried to leave (applied for job and/or interviewed), but the job market keeps me here.
I think about leaving, but there are few positions to apply for in this job market.
I am considering leaving higher education.
I will just endure the problem.
The problem isn't bad enough for me to change jobs.
There are no problems with bullying on my job.
Are there specific strategies you or your organization used to stop a bully?

References

Batsche, G. M., & Knoff, H. M. (1994). Bullies and their victims: Understanding a pervasive problem in schools. *School Psychology Review, 23*, 165–174.

Bonett, D. (2002). Sample size requirements for testing and estimating coefficient Alpha. *Journal of Educational and Behavioral Statistics, 27*(4), 335–340. https://doi.org/10.3102/10769986027004335

Bujang, M. A., Omar, E. D., & Baharum, N. A. (2018). A review on sample size determination for Cronbach's alpha test: A simple guide for researchers. *The Malaysian Journal of Medical Sciences: MJMS, 25*(6), 85–99. https://doi.org/10.21315/mjms2018.25.6.9

Byrne, Z. (2015). *Understanding employee engagement: Theory, research and practice.* Routledge.

Cronbach, L. J. (1951). Coefficient alpha and the internal structure of tests. *Psychometrika, 16*(3), 297–334.

Einarsen, S., Hoel, H., Zapf, D., & Cooper, C. (2011). *Bullying and harassment in the workplace*. CRC Press.

Ercan, I., Yazici, B., Sigirli, D., Ediz, B., & Kan, I. (2007). Examining Cronbach alpha, theta, omega reliability coefficients according to sample size. *Journal of Modern Applied Statistical Methods, 6*(1), 291–303.

Fleiss, J. L. (1986). *Design and analysis of clinical experiments*. New York Wiley.

Graham, S., Bellmore, A., & Juvonen, J. (2003). Peer victimization in middle school: When self- and peer views di-verge. *Journal of Applied School Psychology, 19*, 117–137.

Hawker, D. S. J., & Boulton, M. J. (2000). Twenty years' re- search on peer victimization and psychosocial maladjustment: A meta-analytic review of cross-sectional studies. *Journal of Child Psychology and Psychiatry and Allied Disciplines, 41*, 441–455.

Hertzog, M. A. (2008). Considerations in determining sample size for pilot studies. *Research in Nursing & Health, 31*(2), 180–191.

Hochschild, A. R. (1979). Emotion work, feeling rules, and social structure. *American Journal of Sociology, 85*(3), 551–575.

Hollis, L. P. (2012). *Bully in the ivory tower: How aggression & incivility erode American higher education*. Patricia Berkly LLC.

Hollis, L. P. (2014). Lambs to slaughter? Young people as the prospective target of workplace bullying in higher education. *Journal of Education and Human Development, 3*(4), 45–57.

Hollis, L. P. (2015a). Bully university? The cost of workplace bullying and employee disengagement in American higher education. *Sage Open, 5*(2), 2158244015589997.

Hollis, L. P. (2015b). Take the Bull by the Horns: A structural approach to minimize workplace bullying for women in American higher education. *Public Policy Forum*. Oxford University, pp. 1–12.

Kaltiala-Heino, R., Rimpela, M., Marttunen, M., Rimpela, A., & Rantanen, P. (1999). Bullying, depression, and suicidal ideation in Finnish adolescents: School survey. *British Medical Journal, 319*, 348–351.

Keashly, L., & Neuman, J. H. (2010). Faculty experiences with bullying in higher education: Causes, consequences, and management. *Administrative Theory & Praxis, 32*(1), 48–70.

Ladika, S. (2018). Bullying and cyberbullying: Are schools doing enough to protect victims? *The CQ Researcher, 28*(5), 97–120. http://library.cqpress.com/

Mithaug, D. E. (1996). *Equal opportunity theory*. Sage.

Muschert, G. V., & Peguero, A. A. (2010). The columbine effect and school anti-violence policy. *New Approaches to Social Problems Treatment, 17*, 117–148. https://doi.org/10.1108/S0196-1152(2010)0000017007

Namie, G., & Namie, R. (2009). *The bully at work: What you can do to stop the hurt and reclaim your dignity on the job*. Sourcebooks, Inc.

Nansel, T. R., Haynie, D. L., & Simons-Morton, B. G. (2003). The association of bullying and victimization with middle school adjustment. *Journal of Applied School Psychology, 19*, 45–61.

Notelaers, G., Van der Heijden, B., Hoel, H., & Einarsen, S. (2019). Measuring bullying at work with the short-negative acts questionnaire: Identification of targets and criterion validity. *Work & Stress, 33*(1), 58–75.

Olweus, D. (1994). Bullying at School. In L. R. Huesmann (Ed.), *Aggressive behavior. The Plenum Series in social/clinical psychology*. Springer. https://doi.org/10.1007/978-1-4757-9116-7_5

Oncu, M., Kim, N., & Faith, M. S. (2015). Statistical power as a function of Cronbach alpha of instrument questionnaire items. *BMC Medical Research Methodology, 15*(1), 1–9.

Smith, P. K., Shu, S., & Madsen, K. (2001). Characteristics of victims of school bullying. In *Peer harassment in school: The plight of the vulnerable and victimized* (pp. 332–351). Guilford Press.

Swearer, S. M., Espelage, D. L., Vaillancourt, T., & Hymel, S. (2010). What can be done about school bullying? Linking research to educational practice. *Educational Researcher, 39*(1), 38–47.

Twale, D. J., & De Luca, B. M. (2008). *Faculty incivility: The rise of the academic bully culture and what to do about it* (Vol. 128). John Wiley & Sons.

CHAPTER 4

Confirming Coercion in Community Colleges: A Validated Instrument for Workplace Bullying at Two-Year Institutions (2014)

Abstract Community colleges are understudied when compared to four-year colleges and universities; additionally, workplace bullying is an under-studied phenomenon. Therefore, in order to study workplace bullying in community college, I needed to create an original instrument. After conducting the four-year study in 2012 regarding workplace bullying in higher education for four-year colleges and universities, in 2016, I replicated the *Bully in the Ivory Tower*, which was for four-year colleges and universities [Hollis, *Bully in the ivory tower: How aggression & incivility erode American higher education*. Patricia Berkly LLC (2012)], and applied the same process to community colleges. For this study, I wanted to also examine the impact labor unions have on curtailing workplace bullying. In the resultant book, *The Coercive Community College*, (2016), I used Sidanius and Pratto's [*Social dominance: An intergroup theory of social hierarchy and oppression*. Cambridge University Press (1999)] social dominance theory and Mithaug's [*Equal opportunity theory*. Sage (1996)] equal opportunity theory. I also used public shaming theories from Kerfoot [*Nursing Economics, 25*(4): 233, 234, 227 (2007)] and Gilbert and Proctor [*Clinical Psychology, 13*, 353–379 (2006)]. To examine labor unions, I employed Dawkins's [*Journal of Business Ethics, 95*, 129143 (2010). https://doi.org/10.1007/S10551-009-0342-3] social responsibility theory. The Cronbach's Alpha process is presented step-by-step. The

L. P. Hollis, *Instrumental Social Justice in Higher Education*, https://doi.org/10.1007/978-3-031-49289-1_4

chapter continues with the dissemination procedures and the findings; then the actual instrument is presented. The findings resulted in a book, *The Coercive Community College: Bullying and Its Costly Impact on the Mission to Serve Underrepresented Populations* (2016). Often considered to be the baseline study on workplace bullying and community colleges, the community college book also addresses cyber bullying, students, and the impact on underrepresented populations. The chapter concludes with a discussion of the book, conference presentations, and poster sessions that resulted from the study.

Keywords Community college • Workplace bullying • Instrument development • Cronbach Alpha

MOTIVATION FOR STUDY

After accepting a tenure-track job in a community college leadership doctoral program, I was motivated to complete this study on workplace bullying and community colleges. Many academics recognize that the community college space is an understudied educational sector (David & Kanno, 2021; Godin & Bishop, 2022; Howard et al., 2019; Julien et al., 2022). Further, after my experience working at a community college, I had firsthand knowledge of how community colleges are different than four-year colleges given the unions, budget constraints, and open access mission.

A colleague of mine once said that institutions with money can hide their warts; stated otherwise, institutions that are flush with cash may be in a better position to cover up their problems. Given that community colleges are underfunded, one might anticipate workplace bullying being a bigger issue at the two-year level than at the four-year level.

Further, during my community college experience as the director of academic advising, my staff and I faced grievance, after complaint, after problem with the union, which was retaliating against the vice president of academic affairs. Faculty used the union grievance process to impart chaos on the office. I was one of three directors who only worked for a calendar year before leaving that position. Given my upbringing in Western Pennsylvania, I grew up respecting unions. The collective voice from union members could sway elections and modify work conditions.

However, I didn't think unions should file vexatious grievances to bully middle management.

With my background, direct community college experience, and the research agenda on workplace bullying, I was committed to examining workplace bullying in community college. I found, however, that the comments and reactions from the community college sample were harsher and more frustrated than the data from the four-year study. More respondents complained about their work and even the study, but they completed the survey.

Design and Methods

Similar to the *Bully in the Ivory Tower* study, the Coercive Community College study primarily relied on descriptive statistics and qualitative remarks from open-ended questions. Additionally, the chapter on labor unions used a correlation. As this study occurred early in my establishing my research agenda, the goal was to determine the frequency of workplace bullying for community colleges and also to focus further on diverse populations. Consistent with my initial study, the data confirmed that underrepresented and vulnerable populations reported higher frequencies of workplace bullying. This second study had a stronger focus on diversity issues.

Decision on Sample/Population

Aside from my motivation to conduct a study focusing on community colleges due to my faculty appointment, I was also motivated to learn if labor unions can minimize workplace bullying. During my community college experience, my staff and I faced constant bullying from the union, from the secretarial pool, and from executives. We were truly unprotected in a very contentious educational landscape. Yelling and cursing were common occurrences in meetings. My assistant director endured insomnia and hair loss. Hence, I wondered if the problem was specific to this community college. My previous jobs did not have strong unions; therefore, I also considered if unions help or hurt workplace bullying problems. As a result the sample for this study came from Pennsylvania, Arizona, California, Ohio, New Jersey, and New York because these states had the strongest union presence for community colleges.

DISSEMINATION CYCLE

I relied on a dissemination cycle similar to the four-year instrument study on workplace bullying. For potential respondents to complete the study, they should get an invitation and then three reminders to complete the study. When I utilized this process, the most considerable boost to participation came in the second reminder. Like my first workplace bullying study, I used SurveyMonkey in 2014 and sent the link via email to recruit respondents from states that had unions at their community colleges.

Since I was new to survey distribution via the Internet, I learned the hard way that I could not send close to 3000 emails through AOL, MSN, or Yahoo. The ".com" designation resulted in emailed invitations being blocked by MSN or the various firewalls at colleges and universities led to invitations being undeliverable. Therefore, in early 2014 when I collected the data, I used a mail merge service and the server at the local library, which was more acceptable to educational systems. Specifically, I chose the SendBlaster™ software, which allowed me to send mass emails more likely to bypass college and university firewalls. In later research, I have learned to ask my home institution's IT department to create a safe list of all emails. This means that instead of a series of single emails being sent at once and then being flagged as spam, most emails are part of a safe list. The Gmail-based safe list enables me to send bulk emails without those invitations being caught in firewalls.

After gathering email addresses from publicly accessible websites, I invited community college faculty, staff, and executives to participate. The first invitation was sent in mid-October of 2014. Three reminders were sent to potential respondents, with the last invitation to participate occurring in mid-December of 2014.

CRONBACH'S ALPHA FOR INSTRUMENT

When writing a grant proposal or submitting a paper to a high-end journal, reviewers want to confirm that the data in the study are valid. Since the findings are directly related to the instrument's validity, researchers should take care to tabulate the level of internal consistency for the survey by employing Cronbach's Alpha (Oncu et al., 2015). This is because the Cronbach's Alpha evaluates if the scales in the instrument are closely related. Instruments with stronger statistical power yield more reliable and valid findings.

According to Cronbach (1951), a researcher can use an alpha coefficient method to validate Likert-scale questions; further, Oncu et al. (1995) confirmed that the Cronbach's Alpha process is appropriate for true-false questions. Therefore, assigning Likert-scale values to multiple choice questions and evaluating questions for yes/no outcomes was the process I used for applying Cronbach's Alpha to this instrument.

My validating the instrument included conducting a Cronbach's Alpha tabulation with Excel. Instrument analysis resulting in a Cronbach's Alpha at 0.65 or above is considered sufficient, as 0.65 rounds up to the required 0.7 for acceptable reliability (Bujang et al., 2018). The Cronbach's Alpha at 0.64 or below is not acceptable; if the Cronbach's Alpha coefficient is too low, this means the instrument is not valid and will not result in reliable findings. For example, an instrument with a Cronbach's Alpha of 0.47 would be very weak, and the resulting data would not be reliable. Conversely, an instrument that produced a Cronbach's Alpha of 0.88 would have strong validity and the resulting data would be considered reliable. In short, the closer the relationship among instrument questions, the stronger the instrument is as a whole. The closer the Cronbach's Alpha variable is to 1.0, the more reliable the instrument. The goal of the Cronbach's Alpha is to confirm that the instrument's results are valid and reliable. I used the following steps:

Step 1: Conduct a pilot test to gather complete responses for the Cronbach's Alpha analysis. Researchers have noted a sample of 10 to 40 is required to conduct the Cronbach's Alpha (Bonett, 2002; Fleiss, 1986; Hertzog, 2008), yet the more respondents' answers that are included in the Cronbach's Alpha analysis, the more confident one can be in the Cronbach's Alpha tabulation; I relied upon answers from 70 respondents to create an Excel spreadsheet with the questions in the top columns and the respondents' answers in the rows. Be sure to have the data analysis tool pack included in Excel.

Step 2: For each completed respondent, insert the numeral answer for each question. In this instrument, 21 questions were analyzed. See Fig. 4.1 for how to create and populate the spreadsheet. The instrument's first 12 questions included the informed consent and collected demographic information, such as gender, race, sexual orientation, and salary. Figure 4.1 only shows the Excel sheet for questions 10 through 18, but 70 respondents' answers to 21 questions were put into the spreadsheet.

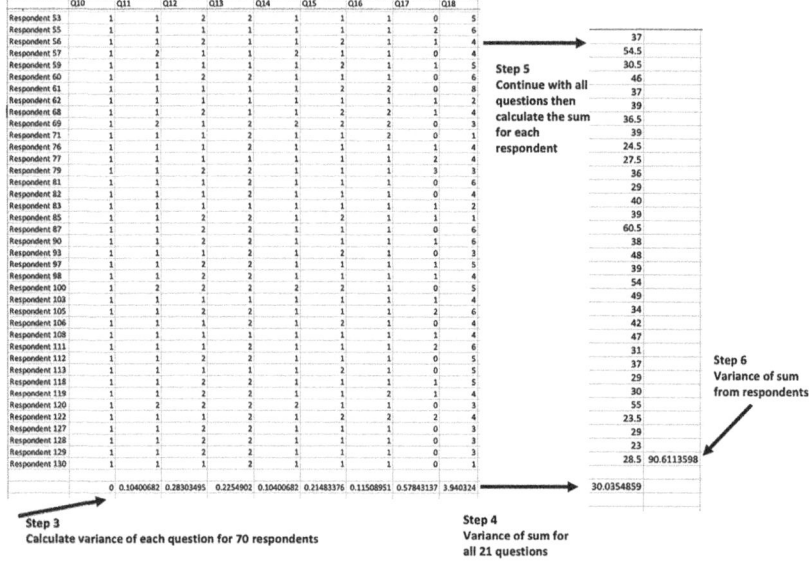

Fig. 4.1   Creating Excel sheet for Cronbach's Alpha analysis

Step 3: Calculate the variance in each question using the variance function: = VAR.S(B2:B70). When Column C was analyzed, the variance = 0.10400682. Similarly, when Column D was analyzed, the variance = 0.28303495. This function should be applied to all columns, resulting in a variance answer for each. For this instrument, 21 variances were tabulated for each of the questions. See Fig. 4.1 for steps three through six to conduct a Cronbach's Alpha.

Step 4: Once the variance for each column is tabulated, the sum of these variances should be tabulated = VAR.S(B70:J70). The sum of variance of all 21 columns = 30.0354859. This is Σs^2_i.

Step 5: Tabulate the sum total for each respondent row. For example, the sum for questions 10 through 33 for Respondent 130 equals 28.5. The sum for Respondent 129 equals 23. Note, for example, Respondents 126, 125, 124, and 123 were skipped because these individuals did not complete the survey.

Step 6: There should now be a final column for the sum of each respondent, represented here in column U. Next, use the variance function to analyze the final sum column = VAR.S(K2:K46) with the resulting variable equaling 90.61. This is $s^2 y$.

Step 7: The Cronbach's Alpha formula is:

$$\alpha = \frac{(n)}{(n-1)} * \frac{\left(s^2_{\,y} - \Sigma s^2_{\,i}\right)}{\left(s^2_{\,y}\right)}$$

N = the number of questions = 21

$$a = \frac{(21)}{(20)} * \frac{\left(90.61\{\text{variance of sum column}\} - 30.035\{\text{sum of variance}\}\right)}{\left(90.61\{\text{variance of sum column}\}\right)}$$

The Cronbach's Alpha for the Coercive Community College instrument = 0.702.

RESULTING PUBLICATIONS

The lengthy survey, which had 21 questions plus demographic questions, led to a solo-authored book on workplace bullying and community colleges. Also, the findings from this study were presented at the American Association of Community Colleges in Chicago (2016). By adding demographic questions about race and gender, the data could support several analyses addressing diversity.

Hollis, L. P. (2016). The Coercive Community College: Bullying and Its Costly Impact on the Mission to Serve Underrepresented Populations. In L. P. Hollis (Ed.), *The Coercive Community College: Bullying and Its Costly Impact on the Mission to Serve Underrepresented Populations* (*Diversity in Higher Education, Vol. 18*) (p. iii), Emerald Group Publishing Limited, Bingley, https://doi.org/10.1108/S1479-364420160000 018021

Please see a list of chapters that this data supported:

1 "Bruising the Bottom Line: Cost of Workplace Bullying and the Compromised Access for Underrepresented Community College Employees" (Hollis, 2016b)
2 "Color Outside the Lines: The Impact of Workplace Bullying on People of Color Working in Community Colleges" (Hollis, 2016c)

3 "Labor Intensive: Workplace Bullying, Union Membership, and Unrealized Civil Rights for People of Color" (Hollis, 2016d)
4 "Socially Dominated: The Racialized and Gendered Positionality of Those Precluded from Bullying" (Hollis, 2016a)
5 "Insult to Injury: The Extent of Bullying for Gender and Sexual Minorities in Community Colleges" (Hollis, 2016e)
6 "Cybershaming—Technology, Cyberbullying, and the Application to People of Color" (Hollis, 2016f)
7 "Stop Bullies in Their Tracks: Bullying Scenarios Reflecting on Underrepresented Groups" (Hollis, 2016g)
8 "Call to Action: Strategies to Create and Maintain Civility for Underrepresented Groups in the Community College" (Hollis, 2016h)

REFLECTIVE QUESTIONS

The book and its chapters are meant to help new and seasoned researchers conduct Cronbach's Alpha for original instruments. Further, the instruments in this book can be used for research; of course, be sure to give the proper citation if one or any of the questions are used or modified for future research. The reflective questions in each chapter are meant to assist instructors in teaching Cronbach's Alpha processes.

1. This chapter reflects on a data collection process that had a specific focus on labor unions. As you consider your study, what compelling elements must you consider so you can recruit a proper sample?
2. To conduct this study specifically in the community college sector, I needed to gather email addresses from public websites. Consider the population you might want to study. How can you get access to them so you can conduct your study?
3. What is the most difficult part of the Cronbach's Alpha process for you? Please identify the issue to discuss with your professor/instructor.
4. This instrument supported a full-length book. How can you develop an instrument that also produces robust data for longer publications?
5. How could you re-cast this instrument to conduct a multiple regression or chi-square? How would you change the questions to collect data appropriate for such an analysis?

APPENDIX: THE INSTRUMENT

The Coercive in Community College (2014)

For the purpose of the study, see the following:

"Bullying" means harassing, offending, socially excluding someone, or negatively affecting someone's work tasks. It occurs repeatedly and regularly, over a period of time. With the escalating process, the person confronted ends up in an inferior position and becomes the target of systematic negative social acts (Einarsen, Hoel, Zapf, & Cooper, 2003).

Does your campus have an explicit anti-bullying policy? (Pick one)

Yes, but no one follows it

No, and no one talks of creating a policy

Yes, it helps maintain peace

Yes, but policy is hard to find (not clear on website or in manual)

No, but we are talking about developing one

Are there Unions/Collective Bargaining Units on your campus?

Yes

No

If there are Unions/Collective Bargaining, are you a member of the union/collective bargaining?

Yes

No

No unions/Collective Bargaining on campus

What best describes your campus regarding ADMINISTRATORS and unions?

Administrators on campus DO have union presence.

Administrators on campus DO NOT have union presence.

What best describes your campus regarding FACULTY and unions?

Faculty DO have union presence.

Faculty DO NOT have union presence.

In regard to bullying at the community college/two-year college... (check all that apply)

I have been bullied in the last 18 months.

I have witnessed bullying in the last 18 months

I have NOT witnessed or experienced bullying in the last 18 months. I have intentionally intimidated and bullied others.

In regard to VICARIOUS bullying (boss sends assistant or other staff to do his/her bullying)...

(check all that apply)

I have been VICARIOUSLY bullied in the last 18 months.

I have witnessed VICARIOUS bullying in the last 18 months.

I have NOT witnessed or experienced VICARIOUS bullying in the last 18 months.

I have intentionally used a subordinate staff member to intimidate and bully others.

In regard to workplace bullying at the community college, how has the UNION been a factor?

No unions on campus

Union ACTS AS BULLY to FACULTY

Union ACTS AS BULLY to ADMINISTRATORS

Union PROTECTS FACULTY from bullying

Union PROTECTS ADMINISTRATION from bullying

Unions exists but play neutral role in regard to bullying

If you have experienced a healthy workplace during your career in community college/two-year college, which factors were significant factors in that healthy work environment?

(Check all that apply)

Positive attitude of boss/supervisor Positive attitude of colleagues Supportive Union

Respect from boss and administration Respect from colleagues

Clear policies supporting a healthy environment Positive interaction with union

Professional development/training that promoted healthy environment Other

In your experience, what is the ORGANIZATIONAL level of the TARGET when bully is SINGLE PERSON?

Your experience means happened to you OR you witnessed it.

(May check two options)

Entry Level/Administrative Support Assistant Director

Director

Non-tenured faculty Tenured Faculty

Assistant or Associate Dean

Dean

Assistant or Associate Vice President/Provost Vice President or Provost

President

I have not witnessed or experienced bullying

Other

In your experience, what is the ORGANIZATIONAL level of the TARGET when bully is THE UNION?

Your experience means happened to you OR you witnessed it.

(May check two options)

Entry Level/Administrative Support Assistant Director

Director

Non-tenured faculty Tenured Faculty

Assistant or Associate Dean

Dean

Assistant or Associate Vice President/Provost Vice President or Provost

President

I have not witnessed or experienced bullying Campus doesn't have unions

Other

Where were the TARGETS bullied?

(Check all that apply)

Individual (one-on-one) meeting In front of students

In front of other staff

In cyberspace (email, chat room, bullet board, etc.)

In local staff meeting

In Union meeting

In division wide or department wide meeting

Other

(Please specify)

In regard to communication, how are TARGETS bullied?

(Check all that apply)

Verbally endured insults and yelling

Verbally endured inappropriate jokes and teasing

Subject to group gossip and rumors.

Face threats of job loss/being fired

Subject to group gossip and rumors.

Excessive union grievances

Ignored, overlooked

Written embarrassment (harsh memos, notes or commands)

Must comply with unreasonable accountability and reporting (minute by minute updates).

Face threats of job loss/being fired.

Harassed by union
Other
(Please specify)
In regard to organizational expectations, how were TARGETS bullied?
(Check all that apply)
Assigned unreasonable deadlines.
Excluded from lunches or other social office gatherings.
Assigned unreasonable tasks.
Union grievance
Must comply with unreasonable accountability and reporting (minute by minute updates).
Their goals or tasks were changed abruptly without notice.
Union Harassment
Their responsibilities, budget or reporting structure were abruptly changed without notice.
Other
(Please specify)
How long did the TARGET endure bullying?
One academic term
Two academic terms
Full calendar year 2–3 calendar years
More than 3 calendar years
Other
How did the TARGET react to being bullied?
(Check up to three options)
Report to supervisors Report to HR
Leave department (transferred internally)
Report to Union
Take more sick time
File grievance with union
Isolate self from group
Resigned/Quit
Other
(Please specify)
Which strategies provided relief for the TARGET (whether yourself or someone you witnessed as a target)?
(Check up to three options)
Report to supervisors

Report to union
Report to HR
Leave department
Take more sick time Isolate self from group
There was no relief
Other
(Please specify)
If bullying occurs in your department or division, how many people have left (or were separated from) the institution in the last 18 months to AVOID the toxic environment?

0
1
2
3
4
5
6
More than 6

In your experience, what is the ORGANIZATIONAL level of the BULLY? Your experience means happened to you OR you witnessed it.
(May check two options)
Entry Level/Admin support
Assistant Director
Director
Non-tenured faculty
Tenured faculty
Union representative
Assistant/Associate Dean
Dean
Assistant or Associate Vice President/Provost Vice President or Provost
President
How did the organization deal with the BULLY?
(Check up to three options)
Did nothing Coached the BULLY
Fired the TARGET
Transferred BULLY to another department
Supported the BULLY
Transferred TARGET to another department

Fired the BULLY
If the UNION is a bully, how did the organization deal with the BULLY?
Did nothing
Removed union bullies in election
Supported Union bully
Empowered Union bully
Union (if there is one on campus) isn't a bully
Follow lead of a good executive unit
Professional development and training
Civility written into performance evaluation Productivity and turnover analysis of department
Other (please specify)
Are there any specific comments or insights you would like to share about workplace bullying in higher education?

References

Bonett, D. (2002). Sample size requirements for testing and estimating coefficient Alpha. *Journal of Educational and Behavioral Statistics, 27*(4), 335–340. https://doi.org/10.3102/10769986027004335

Bujang, M. A., Omar, E. D., & Baharum, N. A. (2018). A review on sample size determination for Cronbach's alpha test: A simple guide for researchers. *The Malaysian Journal of Medical Sciences: MJMS, 25*(6), 85–99. https://doi.org/10.21315/mjms2018.25.6.9

Cronbach, L. J. (1951). Coefficient alpha and the internal structure of tests. *Psychometrika, 16*(3), 297–334.

David, N., & Kanno, Y. (2021). ESL programs at U.S. community colleges: A multistate analysis of placement tests, course offerings, and course content. *TESOL Journal, 12*(2), 1–21. https://doi.org/10.1002/tesj.562

Dawkins, C. (2010). Beyond wages and working conditions: A conceptualization of labor union social responsibilities. *Journal of Business Ethics, 95*, 129143. https://doi.org/10.1007/S10551-009-0342-3

Einarsen, S., Hoel, H., Zapf, D., Cooper, C. (Eds.) (2003). *Bullying and Emotional Abuse in the Workplace: International Perspectives in Research and Practice.* New York, NY: Taylor & Francis.

Fleiss, J. L. (1986). *Design and analysis of clinical experiments.* Wiley.

Gilbert, P., & Procter, S. (2006). Compassionate mind training for people with high shame and self-criticism: Overview and pilot study of a group therapy approach. *Clinical Psychology, 13*, 353–379.

Godin, E., & Bishop, B. (2022). State-level coordination for community college student success. *New Directions for Community Colleges, 2022*(197), 81–92. https://doi.org/10.1002/cc.20499

Hertzog, M. A. (2008). Considerations in determining sample size for pilot studies. *Research in Nursing & Health, 31*(2), 180–191.

Hollis, L. P. (2012). *Bully in the ivory tower: How aggression & incivility erode American higher education.* Patricia Berkly LLC, Wilmington, DE.

Hollis, L. P. (Ed.). (2016). *The coercive community college: Bullying and its costly impact on the mission to serve underrepresented populations.* Emerald Group Publishing.

Hollis, L. P. (2016a). Socially dominated: The racialized and gendered positionality of those precluded from bullying. In *The coercive community college: Bullying and its costly impact on the mission to serve underrepresented populations* (Vol. 18, pp. 103–112). Emerald Group Publishing Limited.

Hollis, L. P. (2016b). Bruising the bottom line: Cost of workplace bullying and the compromised access for underrepresented community college employees. In *The coercive community college: Bullying and its costly impact on the mission to serve underrepresented populations* (Vol. 18, pp. 1–26). Emerald Group Publishing Limited.

Hollis, L. P. (2016c). Color outside the lines: The impact of workplace bullying on people of color working in Community Colleges. In *The Coercive Community College: Bullying and its costly impact on the mission to serve underrepresented populations* (pp. 49–64). Emerald Group Publishing Limited.

Hollis, L. P. (2016d). Labor intensive: Workplace bullying, union membership, and unrealized civil rights for people of color. In *The Coercive Community College: Bullying and its costly impact on the mission to serve underrepresented populations* (pp. 83–101). Emerald Group Publishing Limited.

Hollis, L. P. (2016e). Insult to injury: The extent of bullying for gender and sexual minorities in community colleges. In *The coercive community college: Bullying and its costly impact on the mission to serve underrepresented populations* (pp. 113–123). Emerald Group Publishing Limited.

Hollis, L. P. (2016f). Cybershaming–technology, cyberbullying, and the application to people of color. In *The coercive community college: Bullying and its costly impact on the mission to serve underrepresented populations* (pp. 125–135). Emerald Group Publishing Limited.

Hollis, L. P. (2016g). Stop bullies in their tracks: Bullying scenarios reflecting on underrepresented groups. In *The Coercive Community College: Bullying and its costly impact on the mission to serve underrepresented populations* (Vol. 18, pp. 137–160). Emerald Group Publishing Limited.

Hollis, L. P. (2016h). Call to action: Strategies to create and maintain civility for underrepresented groups in the community college. In *The Coercive Community College: Bullying and its costly impact on the mission to serve underrepresented populations* (Vol. 18, pp. 161–166). Emerald Group Publishing Limited.

Howard, R. M., Potter, S. J., Guedj, C. E., & Moynihan, M. M. (2019). Sexual violence victimization among community college students. *Journal of American College Health,* *67*(7), 674–687. https://doi.org/10.1080/0744848 1.2018.1500474

Julien, H., Gross, M., & Latham, D. (2022). Teaching and its discontents: How academic librarians are negotiating a complicated role. *Journal of Information Literacy, 16*(2), 41–52.

Kerfoot, K. M. (2007). Leadership, civility, and the 'no jerks' rule. *Nursing Economics, 25*(4): 233, 234, 227.

Mithaug, D. E. (1996). *Equal opportunity theory.* Sage.

Oncu, M., Kim, N., & Faith, M. S. (2015). Statistical power as a function of Cronbach alpha of instrument questionnaire items. *BMC Medical Research Methodology, 15*(1), 1–9.

Sidanius, J., & Pratto, F. (1999). *Social dominance: An intergroup theory of social hierarchy and oppression.* Cambridge University Press.

CHAPTER 5

Graduated Validity: Cronbach Alpha Calculations for Graduate Student Workplace Bullying Instrument (2017)

Abstract Through my workplace bullying research, I noticed that employees receive a great deal of research attention, however at the time of the study, little work had been done on graduate students and entry-level faculty. To address conflict and bullying that new research investigators may experience, I created an original instrument to ask how the newer researchers in academia cope with bullying since they are in one of the most vulnerable positions in higher education. The Cronbach Alpha process is presented step-by-step. The chapter continues with the data collection process and the findings; then the actual instrument is presented. The chapter concludes with the peer-reviewed papers and conferences that resulted from the study.

Keywords Workplace bullying • Graduate students • Instrument development • Cronbach Alpha

INSPIRATION/MOTIVATION FOR STUDY

I completed my graduate work at Boston University. Perhaps because it is Martin Luther King's alma mater, or because the faculty were particularly supportive that I had a great doctoral experience. Perhaps from my Pollyanna perspective, I was initially stunned to learn that faculty bully their

L. P. Hollis, *Instrumental Social Justice in Higher Education*, https://doi.org/10.1007/978-3-031-49289-1_5

graduate students. I was also stunned that deans and directors bully the very people they recruit. With these assumptions, I was motivated to conduct this study when a few graduate students at a conference shared that they had been bullied, and how some of their friends gave up on graduate school because of bullying. I could not understand why someone would follow a career in education to abuse others. Consequently, this study moves beyond giving insight about experiences some graduate students and junior faculty endure, the data from this study informed my later work which appeared in a full-length book years later. The success of this study perhaps is that it further supported my workplace bullying research agenda, which led me to consider how graduate students can access ombuds and mentors to move through a combative graduate experience.

Design and Methods

When I conducted this study, I had just begun my research agenda on workplace bullying and I was still developing a series of baseline studies that address workplace bullying. Similar to previous studies of mine from 2012 to 2016, this analysis relied on descriptive statistics and open-ended questions to gather information on the graduate student and entry-level faculty experiences.

RQ1 What is the frequency of workplace bullying for junior faculty and graduate students?
RQ2 Does workplace bullying influence career decisions for junior faculty and graduate students?

As I did not conduct a statistical test, I did not pose a hypothesis. The descriptive statistics were from $n = 257$ graduate students and junior faculty respondents. Respondents also represented different academic disciplines such as Arts and Letters, Social Science, and STEM. Please see (Table 5.1) how respondents reacted.

Table 5.1 Impact bullying has on career trajectory

I tried to leave (applied for job and/or interviewed) 28%
I think about leaving, but there are few positions 44%
I am considering leaving higher education 32%
The problem isn't bad enough for me to leave 26%

Decision on Sample/Population

To recruit graduate students and entry-level faculty, I partnered with a colleague whom I'll refer to by the fictious name Sarah, who hosted a virtual support community for new researchers. During a conversation on another topic, I mentioned my next study about graduate students. Sarah commented that she would be pleased to invite participants from her group. At first glance, this seemed like a great idea. However, Sarah became distracted and was slow in distributing the survey invitations. In other book chapters, I discuss an eight-week data collection window. For this study, I relied on a third party who stalled during data collection. I was pleased to have access to this sample, yet in retrospect found that relying on a third party to distribute the instrument was not as effective as I originally thought. The lesson that I learned and shared with doctoral advisees is not to rely on a third party to recruit a sample. This is especially true during doctoral work when there is a clock ticking for doctoral students to complete the degree. Researchers regardless of experience should use caution in relying on others for the project to be successful. Over the years, I recognize that some graduate programs have their students' profiles and emails publicly available on their departmental website. I probably could have spent six months to visit websites and gather emails, which seems time-consuming. However, I endured a four-month delay in getting Sarah to complete the distribution for invitations to the study. Though there were choices to gather data, this experience confirms that there is no short cut to data collection.

Dissemination Cycle

Because the project depended on a third party to invite participants, I could not engage the typical eight-week data collection window discussed in other chapters. Typically, that cycle includes an initial group invitation sent via email. Next, about every ten days, a reminder is sent to potential participants. The last email is labeled, "Last call to participate." After the original announcement and three reminders, I close the data collection process.

For this study, however, the invitation to participate was sent to members of a graduate student research support group. The support group leader, Sarah, had stated that she hosted graduate students from across the globe; I anticipated that I could conduct a comparative analysis between the United States and other countries. However, the data collection did not result in a robust enough international sample along with the American sample. Because this was not my doctoral work, I had the freedom to re-cast the research questions to properly reflect the respondents' American background. After the initial invitation for Sarah to her group, my col-league lost interest and became noncommunicative for a few months. To complete the study, I needed to remind Sarah of her commitment and insist that the distribution was completed as she once promised. Completing this study proved to be very stressful given the inconsistent recruitment process. Hence, I strongly recommend that researchers who have time constraints such as graduate work or grant deadlines not rely on other people to recruit participants.

CRONBACH ALPHA FOR INSTRUMENT

When writing a grant proposal or submitting a paper to a high-end jour-nal, reviewers want to confirm that the data in the study are valid. Since the findings are directly related to the instrument's validity, researchers should take care to tabulate the level of internal consistency for the survey by employing Cronbach's Alpha (Oncu et al., 2015). This is because the Cronbach Alpha evaluates if the scales in the instrument are closely related. Instruments with stronger statistical power yield more reliable and valid findings.

According to Cronbach (1951), a researcher can use an alpha coeffi-cient method to validate Likert-scale questions; further, Oncu et al., (2015) confirmed that the Cronbach Alpha process is appropriate for true-false questions. Therefore, assigning Likert-scales values to multiple choice questions and evaluating questions for yes/no outcomes was the process I used for applying Cronbach Alpha to this instrument.

My validating the instrument included conducting a Cronbach Alpha tabulation with Excel. Instrument analysis resulting in a Cronbach Alpha at 0.65 or above is considered sufficient as 0.65 rounds up to the required 0.7 for acceptable reliability (Bujang et al., 2018). The Cronbach Alpha at 0.64 or below is not acceptable; if the Cronbach Alpha coefficient is too low, this means the instrument is not valid and will not result in reliable findings.

For example, an instrument with a Cronbach Alpha of 0.47 would be very weak, and the resulting data would not be reliable. Conversely, an instrument that produced a Cronbach Alpha of 0.88 would have strong validity and the resulting data would be considered reliable. In short, the closer the relationship among instrument questions, the stronger the instrument is as a whole. The closer to 1.0 for the Cronbach Alpha variable, the more reliable the instrument. The goal of the Cronbach Alpha is to confirm that the instrument's results are valid and reliable. I used the following steps:

Step 1: Conduct a pilot test to gather at least 20 complete responses for the Cronbach Alpha analysis. Researchers have noted a sample of 10 to 40 is required to conduct the Cronbach Alpha (Bonett, 2002; Fleiss, 1986; Hertzog, 2008); I relied upon answers from 45 respondents. Create an Excel spreadsheet with the questions labeling the top columns and the respondents' answers in the rows. Be sure to have the data analysis tool pack included in Excel. Twenty respondents should be tested.

Step 2: For each completed respondent, insert the numeral answer for each question. In this instrument, 29 questions were analyzed. See Fig. 5.1 for how to create and populate the spreadsheet. The instrument's first 12

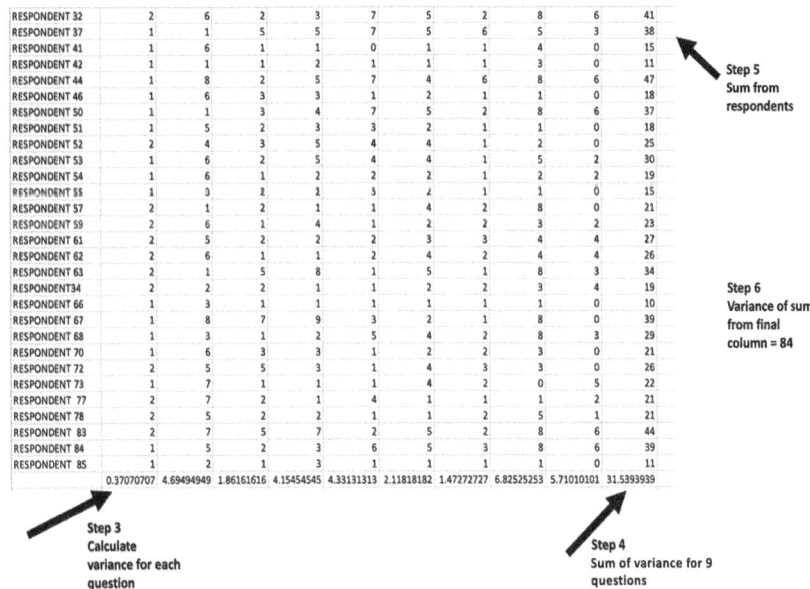

Fig. 5.1   Creating Excel sheet for Cronbach's Alpha analysis

questions included the informed consent and collected demographic information such as gender, race, sexual orientation, and salary. Figure 5.1 only shows the Excel sheet for questions 10 through 17, but 70 respondents' answers are put into the spreadsheet.

Step 3: Calculate the variance in each question using the variance function: = VAR.S(B2:B71).

When column B is analyzed, the variance = 0.3707. Similarly, when column C is analyzed, the variance = 4.6949. This function should be applied to all columns resulting in a variance answer for each. For this instrument, 29 variances were tabulated for each of the questions. See Fig. 5.1 for steps three through six to conduct a Cronbach's Alpha.

Step 4: Once the variance for each column is tabulated, the sum of these variances should be tabulated = VAR.S(B47:J47). The sum of variance of all nine columns = 31.53. This is Σs^2_i.

Step 5: Tabulate the sum total for each respondent row. For example, the sum for questions 10 through 33 for Respondent 3 equals 27. The sum for Respondent 4 equals 34. Note, for example, Respondents 1 and 2 were skipped because the individuals did not complete the survey.

Step 6: There should now be a final column for the sum of each respondent, represented here in column U. Next, use the variance function to analyze the final sum column = VAR.S(K2:K46) with the resulting variable equals 84. This is $s^2 y$.

Step 7: The Cronbach Alpha formula is:

$$\alpha = \frac{(n)}{(n-1)} * \frac{\left(s^2_y - \Sigma s^2_i\right)}{\left(s^2_y\right)}$$

N = the number of questions = 9
Therefore, for the Graduate Student Instrument:

$$\alpha = \frac{(9)}{(8)} * \frac{\left(84\{\text{variance of sum column}\} - 31.54\{\text{sum of variance}\}\right)}{\left(84\{\text{variance of sum column}\}\right)}$$

Resulting Publications

Given the data collection issues and that I typically work on two or three projects simultaneously, I found myself focused on the other projects and only published one article from this data. Since the study was conducted in late 2016 and early 2017, it was one of the earlier studies that I conducted on workplace bullying. Subsequently, the descriptive statistics served as baseline data for later research projects. The open-ended data also provided insight that I used in future work. Comments such as "Coordinator of the department joined the bullying. She is a weak person" or "why recruit people only to haze them when they arrive?" were some of the respondents' comments about bullying. The following publication is a result of this study.

Hollis, L. P. (2017). This is why they leave you: Workplace bullying and insight to junior faculty departure. *British Journal of Education*, *5*(10), 1–7 (Hollis, 2017).

Further, this project yielded other critical lessons about data collection and relying on third parties to advance a research agenda. The success of this project was not just the single publication that emerged, it also informs researchers on possible issues which may require attention to complete the project. Researchers may need to simply restart a project to collect the proper sample when they encounter delays. Additionally, for researchers developing research agendas in nontraditional areas, a study like this also adds to the researcher's knowledge about the field.

Reflective Questions

The book and its chapters are meant to help new and seasoned researchers conduct Cronbach Alpha for original instruments. Further, the instruments in this book can be used for research, yet of course, be sure to give the proper citation if one or any of the questions are used or modified for future research. The reflective questions in each chapter are meant to assist instructors in teaching Cronbach Alpha processes.

1. After reading this chapter, what position do you have about relying on a third party for data collection? In what circumstances might you make an exception to your state position?

2. Just as the researchers for this study branched out to an understudied population to examine workplace bullying, what other or nontraditional populations might you consider when examining your own research area?
3. Why would a researcher conduct a study that primarily relies on descriptive statistics?
4. How can open-ended questions support descriptive statistics in a study?
5. If you designed a study, then lost access to your population, what strategies would you use to continue with the project?

Appendix: Instrument

Graduate Student Workplace Bullying Instrument (2017)

If you have experienced a healthy workplace in higher education (work or graduate schools) which factors were significant factors in that healthy work environment? (Check all that apply)

Positive attitude of boss/supervisor Positive attitude of academic mentor/chair Positive attitude of colleagues

Respect from boss and administration

Respect from colleagues/fellow graduate students Clear policies supporting a healthy environment

Visible Human Resources Department which created healthy environment Recent lawsuit against bully/institution

Recent audit or other external complaint to investigate bully's management Professional development/training that promoted healthy environment

Other

(Please specify)

In your experience, what is the EDUCATIONAL level of the Targets? (May check two options)

High school diploma or equivalent Associates or 2-year degree

Bachelor's degree

Master's degree Doctorate degree

Everyone can be target of cyberbullying.

I have not witnessed or experienced cyberbullying.

Where were the TARGETS cyberbullied?

(Check all that apply if behavior occurred three or more times)

Individual (one-on-one) email Bulk email to entire department

Bulk email which includes students (undergraduates) In list serve or chat room

Facebook cyberbullying

Harassing text to smart phone/cell phone (one-on-one)

Harassing GROUP text smart phone/cell phone

Other

(Please specify)

In regard to communication, how are TARGETS cyberbullied?

(Check all that apply if behavior has occurred three or more times)

Endured insults via one-on-one email

Endured inappropriate jokes and teasing via one-on-one email

Subject to insults and admonishment via GROUP email

Subject to inappropriate jokes and teasing via GROUP email

Rumors and gossip spread in chat rooms,

Facebook or list serve Email requests for information ignored

Endured embarrassment (harsh tone, commands) via email

Use of cursing via email, chat rooms, Facebook to intimidate target

Use of pornography or sexually explicit content via email chat rooms, Facebook to intimidate target

Other

In regard to organizational expectations, how were TARGETS cyberbullied?

(Check all that apply if behavior has occurred three or more times)

Assigned unreasonable professional work deadlines.

Assigned unreasonable academic/research deadlines.

Excluded from lunches or other social office gatherings.

Requests for feedback ignored.

Assigned tasks outside of contract (i.e. you may have a 20 hour a week contract but assigned 35 hours of work)

Their goals or tasks were changed abruptly without notice via email or text.

Superior or advisor steals work without giving you credit.

Other

How long did the TARGET endure cyberbullying?

One academic term

Two academic terms

Full calendar year
2–3 calendar years
More than 3 calendar years
How did the TARGET react to being cyberbullied?
(Check up to three options)
Report to department chair
Report to Human Resources Department/Personnel Department
Leave department
(transferred internally)
If graduate student, transferred to another university
Take more sick time
Isolate self from group
Took extended leave from school or work (more than a month)
Resigned/Quit
Relinquished fellowship
Other
If you are the target of cyberbullying or witness cyberbullying approximately how much time does the target spend strategizing on way to AVOID a cyber bully?
One hour a week
Two hours a week
Three hours a week
Four hours a week
Five hours a week
Six hours a week
Seven hours a week
Eight hours a week
I have not endured or witnessed cyberbullying
If cyberbullying occurs in your department of division, how many people have left (or were separated from) the institution to AVOID the toxic environment?
0
1
2
3
4
5
6
More than 6
No bullying or cyberbullying in my department

REFERENCES

Bonett, D. (2002). Sample size requirements for testing and estimating coefficient alpha. *Journal of Educational and Behavioral Statistics, 27*(4), 335–340. https://doi.org/10.3102/10769986027004335

Bujang, M. A., Omar, E. D., & Baharum, N. A. (2018). A review on sample size determination for Cronbach's alpha test: A simple guide for researchers. *The Malaysian Journal of Medical Sciences: MJMS, 25*(6), 85–99. https://doi.org/10.21315/mjms2018.25.6.9

Cronbach, L. J. (1951). Coefficient alpha and the internal structure of tests. *Psychometrika, 16*(3), 297–334.

Fleiss, J. L. (1986). *Design and analysis of clinical experiments.* Wiley.

Hertzog, M. A. (2008). Considerations in determining sample size for pilot studies. *Research in Nursing & Health, 31*(2), 180–191.

Hollis, L. P. (2017). This is why they leave you: Workplace bullying and insight to junior faculty departure. *British Journal of Education, 5*(10), 1–7.

Oncu, M., Kim, N., & Faith, M. S. (2015). Statistical power as a function of Cronbach alpha of instrument questionnaire items. *BMC Medical Research Methodology, 15*(1), 1–9.

CHAPTER 6

Unclouded Judgment: Using Cronbach Alpha to Validate a Cyberbullying Instrument (2018)

Abstract I conducted this study in late 2017/early 2018 which included faculty and administration in the data collection. To date, few researchers had addressed cyberbullying specifically in higher education. When completing the previous book, *The Coercive Community College*, I recognized a gap in the literature that overall paid little attention to bullying through technology. Given that the data collection included investigating a new area, I found it necessary to create an original instrument. The primary data collection instruments relied on a sample of $n = 734$ faculty and staff. I utilized theories regarding social dominance theory [Ho, A. K., Sidanius, J., Pratto, F., Levin, S., Thomsen, L., Kteily, N., & Sheehy-Skeffington, J. *Personality & Social Psychology Bulletin*, 38(5), 583–606 (2012). https:// doi.org/10.1177/0146167211432765], power, [Brandl, *Generations*, 24(2), 39–45 (2000)] and oppression [Freire, *Pedagogy of the oppressed*. 1968. M. B. Ramos, Trans. Seabury Press (1970)]. The Cronbach's Alpha process is presented step-by-step. The chapter continues with the data collection procedures and the findings; then, the actual instrument is presented. The chapter concludes by discussing the book chapters and conference presentations that resulted from the study.

Keywords Cyberbullying • Instrument development • Cronbach Alpha

© The Author(s), under exclusive license to Springer Nature Switzerland AG 2024
L. P. Hollis, *Instrumental Social Justice in Higher Education*,
https://doi.org/10.1007/978-3-031-49289-1_6

Inspiration/Motivation for Study

I conducted this study after writing several articles and a solo-authored book on workplace bullying and community colleges (Hollis, 2016). At the time of this study, researchers had given little attention to cyberbullying in higher education. A few researchers come to mind, such as Piotrowski (2012) and Manuel (2011). In retrospect, understanding cyberbullying is increasingly important, even before COVID because higher education has shifted more services to cyberspace. Consequently, I was motivated to examine workplace cyberbullying in 2017 to further contribute to a field constantly evolving into virtual instruction and management. I was also interested in social dominance theory and education for underrepresented people (Brandl, 2000; Freire, 1970; Pratto et al., 1994).

Design and Methods

The data from this survey supported several peer-reviewed articles (Hollis, 2019, 2020)—"Abetting bullying," "Bobo doll," "Sleep over it," and "Bullied out of position." The resulting large sample from this student body, $n = 734$, meant the sample was large enough to garner responses from African Americans at a volume that permitted statistical analysis. From the open-ended options, I gathered comments and used Krippendorff's qualitative content analysis (2009).

Decision on Sample/Population

To survey such a large sample, I used email information from Higher Education Publication (HEP), which is produced in Reston, Virginia. This group developed a directory of higher education professionals across the United States. Anyone can purchase contact information such as names, titles, and university or college type. Purchasing the emails for protential respondents meant I did not have to collect publicly available email addresses from college and university websites, a relatively time-consuming endeavor.

Dissemination Cycle

I launched the study at the end of November 2017, which allowed for an initial data collection. After the winter break, I sent three more reminders to potential respondents. In late 2017 and early 2018, I used a software called SendBlaster™ to send email invitations. For later studies, I eliminated the SendBlaster process and used safe lists that an IT department can create for a researcher.

CRONBACH'S ALPHA FOR INSTRUMENT

When writing a grant proposal or submitting a paper to a high-end journal, reviewers want to confirm that the data in the study are valid. Since the findings are directly related to the instrument's validity, researchers should take care to tabulate the level of internal consistency for the survey by employing Cronbach's Alpha (Oncu et al., 2015). This is because the Cronbach's Alpha evaluates if the scales in the instrument are closely related. Instruments with stronger statistical power yield more reliable and valid findings.

According to Cronbach (1951), a researcher can use an alpha coefficient method to validate Likert-scale questions; further, Oncu et al., (1995) confirmed that the Cronbach's Alpha process is appropriate for true-false questions. Therefore, assigning Likert-scale values to multiple choice questions and evaluating questions for yes/no outcomes was the process I used to apply Cronbach's Alpha to this instrument.

My validating the instrument included conducting a Cronbach's Alpha tabulation with Excel. Instrument analysis resulting in a Cronbach's Alpha at 0.65 or above is considered sufficient, as 0.65 rounds up to the required 0.7 for acceptable reliability (Bujang et al., 2018). The Cronbach's Alpha at 0.64 or below is not acceptable; if the Cronbach's Alpha coefficient is too low, this means the instrument is not valid and will not result in reliable findings. For example, an instrument with a Cronbach's Alpha of 0.47 would be very weak, and the resulting data would not be reliable. Conversely, an instrument that produced a Cronbach's Alpha of 0.88 would have strong validity and the resulting data would be considered reliable. In short, the closer the relationship among instrument questions, the stronger the instrument is as a whole. The closer the Cronbach's Alpha variable is to 1.0, the more reliable the instrument. The goal of the Cronbach's Alpha is to confirm that the instrument's results are valid and reliable. I used the following steps:

Step 1: Conduct a pilot test to gather at least 20 complete responses for the Cronbach's Alpha analysis. Researchers have noted a sample of 10 to 40 is required to conduct the Cronbach's Alpha (Bonett, 2002; Fleiss,

1986; Hertzog, 2008); I relied upon answers from 50 respondents. Create an Excel spreadsheet with the questions in the top columns and the respondents' answers in the rows. Be sure to have the data analysis tool pack included in Excel. Twenty respondents should be tested.

Step 2: For each completed respondent, insert the numeral answer for each question. In this instrument, nine questions were analyzed. See Fig. 6.1 for how to create and populate the spreadsheet. The instrument's first 12 questions included the informed consent and collected demographic information such as gender, race, sexual orientation, and salary. Figure 6.1 only shows the Excel sheet for questions 10 through 17, but 50 respondents' answers were put into the spreadsheet.

Step 3: Calculate the variance in each question using the variance function: = VAR.S(B2:B71).

When column B is analyzed, the variance = 1.4489. Similarly, when column C is analyzed, the variance = 0.0723. This function should be applied to all columns, resulting in a variance answer for each. For this instrument, nine variances were tabulated for each of the questions. See Fig. 6.1 for steps three through six to conduct a Cronbach's Alpha.

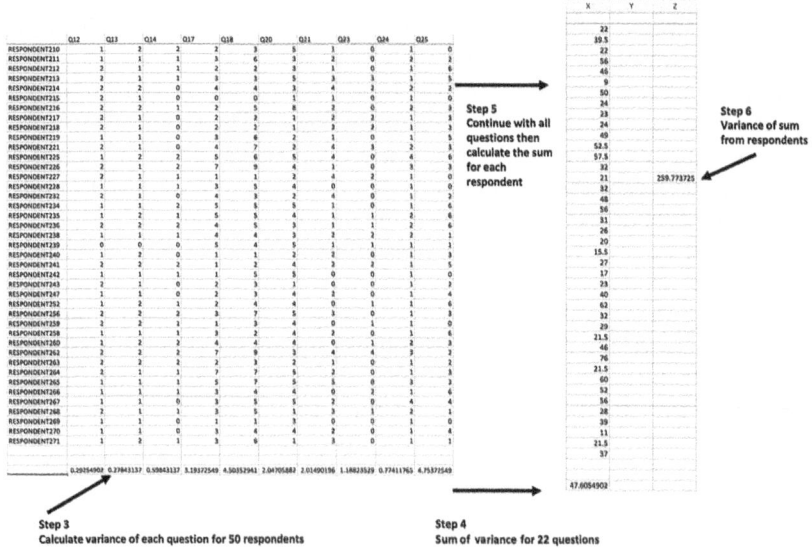

Fig. 6.1 Creating an Excel sheet for Cronbach's Alpha analysis

Step 4: Once the variance for each column is tabulated, the variance of these sums should be tabulated = VAR.S(B55:X55). The sum of variances of all 22 columns = 47.61. This is $\Sigma s^2{}_i$.

Step 5: Tabulate the sum total for each respondent row, for example, the sum for questions 12 through 42. The sum for Respondent 271 equals 37. Note, for example, Respondent 261 was skipped because the individual did not complete the survey.

Step 6: There should now be a final column for the sum of each respondent, represented here in column W. Next, use the sum variance function to analyze the final sum column ==VAR.S(X2:X50), with the resulting variable equaling 49.30. This is $s^2 y$.

Step 7: The Cronbach's Alpha formula is:

$$\alpha = \frac{(n)}{(n-1)} * \frac{\left(s^2{}_y - \Sigma s^2{}_i\right)}{\left(s^2{}_y\right)}$$

N = the number of questions = 22
Therefore, for the Faculty Mentoring:

$$a = \frac{(22)}{(21)} * \frac{\left(\left(259.77\{\text{variance of sum column}\} - 47.61\{\text{sum of variance}\}\right)\right)}{\left(259.77\{\text{variance of sum column}\}\right)}$$

The Cronbach's Alpha for the cyberbullying instrument = 0.855.

RESULTING PUBLICATIONS

Survey research can result in large samples that allow the researcher to answer several research questions. The benefit of a large sample is that it allows the researcher to filter response by race, gender, age, and institution type. Also, with a large sample, the researcher has a better chance of garnering a large enough sample to examine respondents from diverse backgrounds.

Hollis, L. P. (2021a). High-Tech Harassment: A Chi-Squared Confirmation that Workplace Cyberbullying Disproportionally Affects People of Color and the LGBQ Community in Higher Education. In *Human resource perspectives on workplace bullying in higher education: Understanding vulnerable employees' experiences*. Routledge.

Hollis, L. P. (2021b). An Unfair Fight: Black Women's Additional Risk: Facing "Mobbing" in Higher Education In *Human resource perspectives on workplace bullying in higher education: Understanding vulnerable employees' experiences*. Routledge.

Hollis, L. (2019a). The abetting bully: Vicarious bullying and unethical leadership in higher education. *Journal for the Study of Postsecondary and Tertiary Education, 3*, 1–18.

Hollis, L. P. (2019b). Lessons from Bandura's Bobo Doll experiments: Leadership's deliberate indifference exacerbates workplace bullying in higher education. *Journal for the Study of Postsecondary and Tertiary Education, 4*, 085–102.

Hollis, L. P. (2018). Bullied out of position: Black women's complex intersectionality, workplace bullying, and resulting career disruption. *Journal of Black Sexuality and Relationships, 4*(3), 73–89.

REFLECTIVE QUESTIONS

The book and its chapters are meant to help new and seasoned researchers conduct Cronbach's Alpha for original instruments. Further, the instruments in this book can be used for research; of course, be sure to give the proper citation if one or any of the questions are used or modified for future research. The reflective questions in each chapter are meant to assist instructors in teaching Cronbach's Alpha processes.

1. This chapter reflects on a data collection process that had a specific focus on labor unions. As you consider your study, what compelling elements must you consider so you can recruit a proper sample?
2. What is the most difficult part of the Cronbach's Alpha process for you? Please identify the issue to discuss with your professor/instructor.
3. This instrument supported two book chapters and three peer-reviewed articles. How can you develop an instrument that also produces robust data for longer publications?
4. How could you re-cast this instrument to conduct a multiple regression or chi-square? How would you change the questions to collect data appropriate for such an analysis?

Appendix: The Instrument

Cyberbullying Instrument (2018)

Bullying and cyberbullying are serious and costly problems in higher education. We need your help to inform policy development and develop strategies to stop workplace abuse.

This study has two segments:

1). The first set of questions will reflect on bullying, that is face-to-face bullying.

2). The second set of questions will reflect on cyberbullying, bullying using technology.

Does your campus have an explicit anti-bullying policy?

May choose up to 2 options.

Yes, but no one follows it.

No, and no one talks about creating one.

Yes, it helps to maintain the peace.

Yes, but policy is hard to find and/or unclear.

No, but we are talking about developing one.

Yes, but it does not protect against cyberbullying off campus.

Other (please specify)

Note the definition of bullying:

[Workplacebullying] is: harassing, offending, socially excluding someone, or negatively affecting someone's work tasks. This behavior occurs repeatedly and regularly over a period of time. With the escalating process, the person confronted ends up in an inferior position (Einarsen, Hoel, Zapf, & Cooper, 2011, p. 22).

In regard to bullying in the higher education...

(Check all that apply)

I have been bullied in the last 2 years.

I have witnessed bullying in the last 2 years.

I have NOT witnessed or experienced bullying in the last 2 years. I have intentionally intimidated and bullied others.

While, not in last 2 years, I have been target of bullying during my career higher education.

In regard to VICARIOUS bullying (boss sends assistant or other staff to do his/her bullying) in higher education...

(Check all that apply)

I have been VICARIOUSLY bullied in the last 2 years. (1)

I have witnessed VICARIOUS bullying in the last 2 years. (1)

I have NOT witnessed or experienced VICARIOUS bullying in the last 2 years. (0)

I have intentionally used a subordinate staff member to intimidate and bully others. (1)

While, not in last 2 years, I have been target of VICARIOUS bullying during my career higher education. (1)

A TARGET is the person being hurt by the bully.

In regard to organizational expectations, how were TARGETS bullied? (Check all that apply)

Assigned unreasonable deadlines.

Excluded from lunches or other social office gatherings.

Assigned unreasonable tasks.

Must comply with unreasonable accountability and reporting (minute by minute updates).

Unfairly denied promotion or advancement opportunities.

Their goals or tasks were changed abruptly without notice.

Their responsibilities, budget or reporting structure were abruptly changed without notice.

Other (please specify)

In regard to communication, how are TARGETS bullied?

(Check all that apply)

Verbally endured insults and yelling

Verbally endured inappropriate jokes and teasing

Subject to group gossip and rumors.

Face threats of job loss/being fired

Subject to group gossip or rumors

Ignored, overlooked

Written embarrassment (which are not email) such as harsh memos, notes or commands

Face threats of being demoted

Must comply with unreasonable accountability and reporting (minute by minute updates)

Other (please specify)

How long did the TARGET endure BULLYING?

One academic term

Two academic terms

Full calendar year

2–3 calendar years

More than 3 calendar years

Which strategies provided relief for the TARGET from BULLYING (whether yourself or someone you witnessed as a target)?

(Check up to three options)

Report to supervisors

Report to HR

Leave department

Responded in kind (bullied back)

Report to EEO Department (internal or external)

Take more sick time

Isolate self from group

There was no relief

Other (please specify)

Are there specific strategies you or your organization used to stop a BULLY?

Enforcing a zero tolerance/anti-bullying policy

Follow lead of a good executive unit

Professional development and training

Civility written into performance evaluation

Productivity and turnover analysis of department

Recent state legislation prohibiting workplace abuse

None

Other (please specify)

How did the organization deal with the BULLY?

(Check up to three options)

Did nothing

Coached the BULLY

Fired the TARGET

Transferred BULLY to another department

Supported the BULLY

Transferred TARGET to another department

Fired the BULLY

If bullying occurs in your department or division, how many people have left (or were separated from) the institution in the last 3 years to AVOID the toxic environment?

0

1

2

3

4

5

6

More than 6

Think of your career in higher education. Have you left an institution of higher learning to avoid a BULLY or effect of a BULLY on staff?

Yes

No

We will now move to CYBERBULLYING: Note the definition of CYBERBULLYING:

Cyberbullying is defined as "the process of using the Internet, cell phones, or other devices to send or post text or imagines intended to hurt or embarrass another person" (National Crime Prevention Council, 2012). Other definitions include … inappropriate, unwanted social exchange behaviors initiated by a perpetrator via online or wireless communication technology and devices. The unwanted social exchange occurs over a period of time, in attempts to shame, belittle, or harass the target.

In regard to CYBERBULLYING in higher education… (Check all that apply)

I have been the target of cyberbullying in the last 2 years in higher education.

I have a colleague who has been the target of cyberbullying in the last 2 years in higher education

I have NOT been a target or had a colleague who has been target of cyberbullying in last 2 years in higher education.

I have intentionally used cyberbullying to intimidate others in higher education.

While not in last 2 years, I have been target of cyberbullying during my career or educational experiences in higher education.

The TARGET is a person hurt in cyberspace by cyberbully

In regard to communication, how are TARGETS cyberbullied?

(Check all that apply if behavior has occurred three or more times)

Endured insults via one-on-one email

Endured inappropriate jokes and teasing via one-on-one email

Subject to insults and admonishment via GROUP email

Subject to inappropriate jokes and teasing via GROUP email

Rumors and gossip spread in chat rooms, Facebook or list serve

Email requests for information ignored

Endured embarrassment (harsh tone, commands) via email

Use of cursing via email, chat rooms, Facebook to intimidate target

Use of pornography or sexually explicit content via email chat rooms, Facebook to intimidate target

I have not witnessed cyberbullying

Other (please specify)

Where were the TARGETS cyberbullied?

(Check all that apply if behavior has occurred three more times).

Individual (one-on-one) email Bulk email to entire department

Bulk email which includes students

In list serve or chat room

Facebook cyberbullying (or other platform like LinkedIn) Harassing text to smart phone/cell phone (one-on-one) Harassing GROUP text to smart phone/cell phone

I have not witnessed cyberbullying

Other (please specify)

If you have been the TARGET of CYBERBULLYING...did the cyberbullying follow you to your personal space?

(Check all that apply)

Yes, I have been targeted on **Facebook**

Yes, I have been targeted on **holiday break**

Yes, I have been targeted during **summer break**

Yes, I have been targeted during **evening hours**

Yes, I have been targeted while at **conferences**

Yes, I have been targeted on **weekends**

Yes I have been targeted on **LinkedIn**

Yes, I have been targeted on **Twitter**

Yes, I have been targeted, but **ONLY AT WORK**

No, I have NOT been targeted in any cyberbullying

Which strategies provided relief for the TARGET of CYBERBULLYING (whether yourself or someone you witnessed as a target)?

(Check up to three options)

Report to supervisors

Report to HR

Respond in kind (bully back through cyberspace)

Leave department

Report to EEO Department (internal or external)

Block the cyberbully in email

Take more sick time

Isolate self from group

Delete your own online account such as Facebook or LinkedIn

There was no relief

Other (please specify)

How long did the TARGET endure CYBERBULLYING?

One academic term Two academic terms

Full calendar year

2–3 calendar years

More than 3 calendar years

I have not witnessed cyberbullying

If you are the target of CYBERBULLYING or witnessed CYBERBULLYING, approximately how much time does the target spend strategizing on ways to AVOID the CYBERBULLY?

One hour a week

Two hours a week

Three hours a week

Four hours a week

Five hours a week

Six hours a week

A full day total over a week

I have not endured or witnessed CYBERbullying

If CYBERBULLYING occurs in your department or division, how many people have left (or were separated from) the institution in the last 3 years to AVOID the toxic environment?

0

1

2

3

4

5

6

More than 6

Think of your career in higher education. Have you left an institution of higher learning to avoid CYBERBULLYING or effect of CYBERBULLYING on staff?

Yes

No

Are there specific strategies you or your organization used to stop a CYBERBULLY?

Enforcing a zero tolerance/anti-bullying policy

Follow lead of a good executive unit

Professional development and training
Civility written into performance evaluation
Deny cyberbully's access to institution's Internet/email
Productivity and turnover analysis of department
Recent state legislation prohibiting workplace abuse
None
Other
(Please specify)
How did the organization deal with the CYBERBULLY?
(Check up to three options)
Did nothing
Coached the CYBERBULLY
Restricted cyberbully's access to network
Fired the TARGET
Transferred CYBERBULLY to another department
Supported the CYBERBULLY
Order CYBERBULLY to delete online account (i.e. Facebook, LinkedIn)
Transferred TARGET to another department
Fired the CYBERBULLY
Do you have any other comments about BULLYING or CYBERBULLYING in higher education?

REFERENCES

Bonett, D. (2002). Sample size requirements for testing and estimating coefficient alpha. *Journal of Educational and Behavioral Statistics, 27*(4), 335–340. https://doi.org/10.3102/10769986027004335

Brandl, B. (2000). Power and control: Understanding domestic abuse in later life. *Generations, 24*(2), 39–45.

Bujang, M. A., Omar, E. D., & Baharum, N. A. (2018). A review on sample size determination for Cronbach's alpha test: A simple guide for researchers. *The Malaysian Journal of Medical Sciences: MJMS, 25*(6), 85–99. https://doi.org/10.21315/mjms2018.25.6.9

Cronbach, L. J. (1951). Coefficient alpha and the internal structure of tests. *Psychometrika, 16*(3), 297–334.

Einarsen, S., Hoel, H., Zapf, D., & Cooper, C. L. (2011). The Concept of Bullying and Harassment at Work: The European Tradition. In S. Einarsen, H. Hoel, D. Zapf, & C. L. Cooper (Eds.), *Bullying and harassment in the workplace: Developments in theory, research, and practice.*

Fleiss, J. I. (1986). *The design and analysis of clinical experiments.* New York Wiley.

Freire, P. (1970). *Pedagogy of the oppressed*. 1968. M. B. Ramos, Trans. Seabury Press.

Hertzog, M. A. (2008). Considerations in determining sample size for pilot studies. *Research in Nursing & Health, 31*(2), 180–191.

Hollis, L. P. (Ed.). (2016). *The coercive community college: Bullying and its costly impact on the mission to serve underrepresented populations*. Emerald Publishing Limited.

Hollis, L. P. (2018). Bullied out of position: Black women's complex intersectionality, workplace bullying, and resulting career disruption. *Journal of Black Sexuality and Relationships, 4*(3), 73–89.

Hollis, L. P. (2019a). The abetting bully: Vicarious bullying and unethical leadership in higher education. *Journal for the Study of Postsecondary and Tertiary Education, 3*, 1–18.

Hollis, L. P. (2019b). Lessons from Bandura's Bobo Doll experiments: Leadership's deliberate indifference exacerbates workplace bullying in higher education. *Journal for the Study of Postsecondary and Tertiary Education, 4*, 085–102.

Hollis, L. P. (2020). Brown and Bullied Around: The Relationship between Colorism and Workplace Bullying for African Americans/ Blacks. In Kamilah Woodson (Ed.), *Colorism then, now, & tomorrow: Refining a global phenomenon with implication for policy, research and practice* (pp. 158–173). Fielding University Press.

Hollis, L. P. (2021a). High-tech harassment: A chi-squared confirmation that workplace cyberbullying disproportionally affects people of color and the LGBQ community in higher education. In *Human resource perspectives on workplace bullying in higher education: Understanding vulnerable employees' experiences*. Routledge.

Hollis, L. P. (2021b). An unfair fight: Black women's additional risk: Facing "Mobbing" in higher education. In *Human resource perspectives on workplace bullying in higher education: Understanding vulnerable employees' experiences*. Routledge.

Krippendorff, K. (2009). *The content analysis reader*. Sage.

Manuel, N. R. (2011). Cyber-bullying: Its recent emergence and needed legislation to protect adolescent victims. *Loyola Journal of Public Interest Law, 13*(1), 219–225.

National Crime Prevention Council. (2012). *What is cyberbullying*. Washington DC. https://www.stopbullying.gov/cyberbullying/what-is-it

Oncu, M., Kim, N., & Faith, M. S. (2015). Statistical power as a function of Cronbach alpha of instrument questionnaire items. *BMC Medical Research Methodology, 15*(1), 1–9.

Piotrowski, C. (2012). From workplace bullying to cyberbullying: The enigma of harassment in modern organizations. *Organizational Development Journal, 30*(4), 44–53.

Pratto, F., Sidanius, J., Stallworth, L. M., & Malle, B. F. (1994). Social dominance orientation: A personality variable predicting social and political attitudes. *Journal of Personality and Social Psychology, 67*(4), 741.

CHAPTER 7

The Valid Voices of Human Resources Professionals: Addressing with Workplace Bullying from the Human Resources Perspective (2021)

Abstract After ten years of conducting workplace bullying research, I noticed that human resources departments are typically vilified regarding their response to reported workplace bullying. Common questions such as the impact of an ombudsperson and the impact of the organizational structure were central research questions in various studies. Also, workplace bullying disproportionally affects women and people of color. In turn, this chapter reviews how survey design and the resulting data were at the foundation of the full-length book *Human Resource Perspectives on Workplace Bullying in Higher Education: Understanding Vulnerable Employees' Experiences* (2021). The primary data collection instruments relied on a sample of $n = 245$ human resources professionals. I utilized theories regarding abuse and power [Grossman, *Boston University Law Review, 95*, 1029–1048 (2015)], Bolman and Deal's [*Reframing organizations: Artistry, choice, and leadership.* John Wiley & Sons (2017)] organizational structure theories, and other bureaucratic theorists including Manning [*Organizational theory in higher education.* Routledge (2017)], Northouse [*Leadership: Theory and Practice.* Sage Publications (2021)], and Weber et al. [*From Max Weber: Essays in Sociology: Essays in Sociology.* Oxford University Press (1946)]. The Cronbach's Alpha process is presented step-by-step. The chapter continues with the data collection procedures and the findings; then the actual instrument is presented. The chapter concludes by discussing the book chapters and conference presentations that resulted from the study.

Keywords Higher education • Human resources • Workplace bullying • Instrument development

INSPIRATION/MOTIVATION FOR STUDY

I conducted this study after writing several articles and a solo-authored book on workplace bullying and community colleges (Hollis, 2016). Throughout much of the literature, human resources personnel are vilified for not understanding workplace bullying (Cowan, 2012; Harrington et al., 2015), not caring about workplace bullying (Lewis & Rayner, 2002), or not being trained to handle workplace bullying. Consequently, I was motivated to go straight to the source and ask human resources about their experiences and training. Many HR professionals reported being bullied themselves. Others commented that their institution just did not charge them with managing workplace bullying. I also recognized that bureaucratic and leadership structures influence the workplace bullying problem (Bolman & Deal, 2017; Weber et al., 1946). Apathetic or distracted leadership is at the root of institutions not empowering HR to address workplace bullying (Northouse, 2000). While the problem about an institution's apathetic response to bullying might appear to emanate from human resources, the study confirmed that human resources personnel are just part of a larger system that dictates to them as well.

DESIGN AND METHODS

The data from this survey supported several chapters of *Human Resources Perspectives* (Hollis, 2021a). From the open-ended options, I gathered comments and used Krippendorff's qualitative content analysis (2009). Three other chapters utilized chi-square analysis.

Decision on Sample/Population

To understand the human resources professionals' perspective, I choose human resources directors, associate directors, assistant directors, chief diversity officers, and ombudspersons for the sample. This population would know how human resources make decisions about workplace bully-ing intervention or know why interventions are not implemented at their respective institutions. To create research that accurately represented the sample in question, human resources professionals, I found it prudent to query them directly.

Dissemination Cycle

Though any human resources unit will have onboarding activities, in higher education, the summers present fewer distractions for administra-tors. To collect the data, I used the Higher Education Publication (HEP), a directory which provides contact information for higher education per-sonnel at the director level or higher. With these email addresses, I asked our IT department to create a safe list for all the emails. Next, I sent the invitation to participate to the safe list of human resources personnel. The first invitation went out during the last week of June 2018. I sent three more in ten-day intervals. The resulting sample was $n = 245$.

CRONBACH'S ALPHA FOR INSTRUMENT

When writing a grant proposal or submitting a paper to a high-end jour-nal, reviewers want to confirm that the data in the study are valid. Since the findings are directly related to the instrument's validity, researchers should take care to tabulate the level of internal consistency for the survey by employing Cronbach's Alpha (Oncu et al., 2015). This is because the Cronbach's Alpha evaluates if the scales in the instrument are closely related. Instruments with stronger statistical power yield more reliable and valid findings.

According to Cronbach (1951), a researcher can use an alpha coeffi-cient method to validate Likert-scale questions; further, Oncu et al. (2015) confirmed that the Cronbach's Alpha process is appropriate for true-false questions. Therefore, assigning Likert-scale values to multiple choice questions and evaluating questions for yes/no outcomes was the process I used for applying Cronbach's Alpha to this instrument.

My validating the instrument included conducting a Cronbach's Alpha tabulation with Excel. Instrument analysis resulting in a Cronbach's Alpha at 0.65 or above is considered sufficient, as 0.65 rounds up to the required 0.7 for acceptable reliability (Bujang et al., 2018). The Cronbach's Alpha at 0.64 or below is not acceptable; if the Cronbach's Alpha coefficient is too low, this means the instrument is not valid and will not result in reliable findings. For example, an instrument with a Cronbach's Alpha of 0.47 would be very weak, and the resulting data would not be reliable. Conversely, an instrument that produced a Cronbach's Alpha of 0.88 would have strong validity and the resulting data would be considered reliable. In short, the closer the relationship among instrument questions, the stronger the instrument is as a whole. The closer to 1.0 for the Cronbach's Alpha variable, the more reliable the instrument is. The goal of the Cronbach's Alpha is to confirm that the instrument's results are valid and reliable. I used the following steps:

Step 1: Conduct a pilot test to gather at least 20 complete responses for the Cronbach's Alpha analysis. Researchers have noted a sample of 10 to 40 is required to conduct the Cronbach's Alpha (Bonett, 2002; Fleiss, 1986; Hertzog, 2008); I relied upon answers from 50 respondents. Create an Excel spreadsheet with the questions labeling the top columns and the respondents' answers in the rows. Be sure to have the data analysis tool pack included in Excel.

Step 2: For each completed respondent, insert the numeral answer for each question. In this instrument, 12 questions were analyzed. See Fig. 7.1 for how to create and populate the spreadsheet. The instrument's first 12

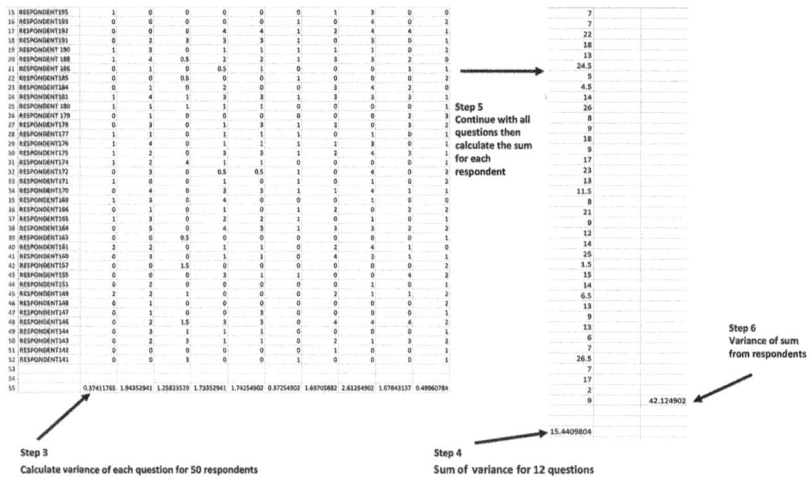

Fig. 7.1   Creating Excel sheet for Cronbach's Alpha analysis

questions included the informed consent and collected demographic information such as gender, race, sexual orientation, and salary. Figure 7.1 only shows the Excel sheet for questions 10 through 20.

Step 3: Calculate the variance in each question using the variance function: = VAR.S(B2:B55).

When Column B is analyzed, the variance = 0.37411765. Similarly, when Column C is analyzed, the variance = 1.94352941. This function should be applied to all columns, resulting in a variance answer for each. For this instrument, 12 variances were tabulated for each of the questions. See Fig. 7.1 for steps three through six to conduct a Cronbach's Alpha.

Step 4: Once the variance for each column is tabulated, the variance of these sums should be tabulated = VAR.S(B52:M52). The sum of variances of all 12 columns = 15.44. This is $\Sigma s^2{}_i$.

Step 5: Tabulate the sum total for each respondent row. For example, the sum for questions 12 through 18 for Respondent 141 equals 9. The sum for respondent 142 equals 2. Note, for example, Respondent 150 was skipped because the individual did not complete the survey.

Step 6: There should now be a final column for the sum of each respondent, represented here in column K. Next, use the sum variance function to analyze the final sum column ==VAR.S(K2:K50), with the resulting variable equaling 42.12. This is s^2y.

Step 7: The Cronbach's Alpha formula is:

$$\alpha = \frac{(n)}{(n-1)} * \frac{\left(s^2{}_y - \Sigma s^2{}_i\right)}{\left(s^2{}_y\right)}$$

Therefore, for the human resources instrument:

$$a = \frac{(12)}{(11)} * \frac{\left(\left(42.12\,\{\text{variance of sum column}\} - 15.44\,\{\text{sum of variance}\}\right)\right)}{\left(42.12\,\{\text{variance of sum column}\}\right)}$$

Alpha = 0.69.

Resulting Publications

The instrument supplied enough data for five chapters in *Human Resources Perspectives* (Hollis & Yamada, 2021):

Hollis, L. P. (2021). Training Current HR Personnel for New Tricks Analyzing the Relationship Between Training and Workplace Bullying. (Ed. Hollis, L. P.) *Human resource perspectives on workplace bullying in higher education: Understanding vulnerable employees' experiences.* Routledge. (Hollis, 2021a)

Hollis, L. (2021). Speaking for themselves the voices of human resources personnel regarding workplace bullying in higher education. (Ed. Hollis, L. P.) *Human resource perspectives on workplace bullying in higher education: Understanding vulnerable employees' experiences.* Routledge. (Hollis, 2021b)

Hollis, L. (2021). Is Bullying Baked into the University? The Organizational Placement of Human Resources and Its Relationship with Workplace Bullying. (Ed. Hollis, L. P.) *Human resource perspectives on workplace bullying in higher education: Understanding vulnerable employees' experiences.* Routledge. (Hollis, 2021c)

Hollis, L. P. (2021). Bullied About? Lawyer Up! When Workplace Bullying Evolves into Legal Complaints. *Lawyer Up.* (Ed. Hollis, L. P.) *Human resource perspectives on workplace bullying in higher education: Understanding vulnerable employees' experiences.* Routledge. (Hollis, 2021d)

Hollis, L. P. (2021). Ombudsmen as Potential Peacemakers with Workplace Bullying in Higher Education. (Ed. Hollis, L. P.) *Human resource perspectives on workplace bullying in higher education: Understanding vulnerable employees' experiences.* Routledge. (Hollis, 2021e)

Additionally, I presented the data in a 90-minute book launch with Rutgers University. The publisher, Routledge, donated three books for a raffle. I also presented data from one of the chapters for the International Association of Workplace Bullying and Harassment (IAWBH) in Dubai.

REFLECTIVE QUESTIONS

The book and its chapters are meant to help new and seasoned researchers conduct Cronbach's Alpha for original instruments. Further, the instruments in this book can be used for research; of course, be sure to give the proper citation if one or any of the questions are used or modified for future research. The reflective questions in each chapter are meant to assist instructors in teaching Cronbach's Alpha processes.

1. This chapter reflects on a data collection process that had a specific focus, workplace bullying, and HR. As you consider your study,

what compelling elements must you consider so you can recruit a proper sample?

2. This instrument supports three chapters. How can you design an instrument that yields data on two or three related issues?

3. What is the most difficult part of the Cronbach's Alpha process for you? Please identify the issue to discuss with your professor/instructor.

4. Think about potential misnomers in your academic discipline. How can survey research help you clarify such inconsistencies in your field?

5. How could you re-cast this instrument to conduct a multiple regression analysis? How would you change the questions to collect data appropriate for such an analysis?

Appendix: The Instrument

Workplace Bullying from the Human Resources Perspective (2021)

Do you personally attend local training for human resources? (Check all that apply)

EEOC rules training

Department of Justice training

SHRM training

Conferences on HR specifically

No training

Other (please specify)

Does your school have ombudsman or ombuds department?

Yes, one person. The position has been functioning UNDER FOUR years

Yes, one person. The position has been functioning at least FIVE years

Yes, one person. The position has been functioning at least TEN years

Yes, one person. The position has been functioning at least FIFTEEN years

Yes, an OFFICE of two or more has been functioning UNDER FOUR years

Yes, an OFFICE of two or more has been functioning least FIVE years

Yes, an OFFICE of two or more has been functioning least TEN years

Yes, an OFFICE of two or more has been functioning least FIFTEEN years

No, we have no ombudsman or ombuds department

How often does HR have professional internal training about employees' rights?
Every six months
Every year
Every two years
Intermittent
No training in last three years
Other (please specify)
How often do supervisors and managers have professional internal training about employees' rights?
Every six months
Every year
Every two years
Intermittent
No training in last three years
Other (please specify)
Is training for managers and supervisors MANDATORY?
YES, it's mandatory
NO, it's NOT mandatory
Definition of workplace bullying:
[Workplace-bullying] is harassing, offending, socially excluding someone or negatively affecting someone's work tasks. This behavior occurs repeatedly and regularly over a period of time. With the escalating proves, the person confronted ends up in an inferior position (Einarsen, Hoel, Zapf & Cooper, 2011, p. 22).
Does your school have a policy that prohibits harassment by explicitly using the words "workplace bullying?"
No—no policy explicitly using words "workplace bullying"
YES and in place 1–3 years
YES and in place 4–6 years
YES and in place 7–10 years
YES and in place 11+ years
Other (please specify)
Which phrase best fits how HR staff is trained about workplace bullying?
HR is trained specifically on how to deal with workplace bullying
HR handles workplace bullying and Title VII harassment the same
HR recognizes workplace bullying is still legal, so we don't train on it
HR personnel read up on workplace bullying when we have the chance

HR personnel know it's an issue—but we just don't train on it

Other (please specify)

How many managers and supervisors are trained to handle workplace bullying?

More than 75% of managers and supervisors are trained specifically on how to deal with workplace bullying

50%–74% of managers and supervisors are trained specifically on how to deal with workplace bullying

25%–49% of managers and supervisors are trained specifically on how to deal with workplace bullying

Less than 24% of managers and supervisors are trained specifically on how to deal with workplace bullying

I don't know how many are trained

Workplace bullying is not a priority for our institution

Other (please specify)

Do you conduct exit interviews when staff and faculty leave?

It's a mandatory part of our separation process for both faculty and staff.

We only conduct exit interviews with faculty.

We only conduct exit interviews with staff.

Only if the exiting person volunteers.

We do not conduct any exit interviews.

Other (please specify)

Do you know where the bullies are in your organization?

Absolutely, everyone knows

HR/EEO has an idea about where bullies are.

HR/EEO has no idea

Have workplace bullying problems escalated to external complaints with EEOC, Office of Civil Rights, Department of Labor, Whistleblower, or State-Level Human Rights Commission?

(Check all that apply)

Issue escalated to an EEOC complaint

Issue escalated to an OFFICE OF CIVIL RIGHTS complaint

Issue escalated to a DEPARTMENT OF LABOR complaint

Issue escalated to a WHISTLEBLOWER complaint

Issue escalated to STATE LEVEL HUMAN RIGHTS COMMISSION complaint

N/A

Other (please specify)

Reflect on your career in human resources. What other insights do you have regarding human resources and workplace bullying in higher education?

REFERENCES

Bolman, L. G., & Deal, T. E. (2017). *Reframing organizations: Artistry, choice, and leadership*. John Wiley & Sons.

Bonett, D. (2002). Sample size requirements for testing and estimating coefficient alpha. *Journal of Educational and Behavioral Statistics, 27*(4), 335–340. https://doi.org/10.3102/10769986027004335

Bujang, M. A., Omar, E. D., & Baharum, N. A. (2018). A review on sample size determination for Cronbach's alpha test: A simple guide for researchers. *The Malaysian journal of medical sciences: MJMS, 25*(6), 85–99. https://doi.org/10.21315/mjms2018.25.6.9

Cowan, R. L. (2012). It's complicated: Defining workplace bullying from the human resource professional's perspective. *Management Communication Quarterly, 26*(3), 377–403.

Cronbach, L. J. (1951). Coefficient alpha and the internal structure of tests. *Psychometrika, 16*(3), 297–334.

Fleiss, J. L. (1986). *Design and analysis of clinical experiments*. Wiley.

Grossman, J. L. (2015). Moving forward looking back: A retrospective on sexual harassment law. *Boston University Law Review, 95*, 1029–1048.

Harrington, S., Warren, S., & Rayner, C. (2015). Human resource management practitioners' responses to workplace bullying: Cycles of symbolic violence. *Organization, 22*(3), 368–389.

Hertzog, M. A. (2008). Considerations in determining sample size for pilot studies. *Research in Nursing & Health, 31*(2), 180–191.

Hollis, L. P. (Ed.). (2016). *The coercive community college: Bullying and its costly impact on the mission to serve underrepresented populations*. Emerald Group Publishing.

Hollis, L. P. (2021a). Training current HR personnel for new tricks analyzing the relationship between training and workplace bullying. In L. P. Hollis (Ed.), *Human resource perspectives on workplace bullying in higher education: Understanding vulnerable employees' experiences*. Routledge.

Hollis, L. P. (2021b). Speaking for themselves the voices of human resources personnel regarding workplace bullying in higher education. In L. P. Hollis (Ed.), *Human resource perspectives on workplace bullying in higher education: Understanding vulnerable employees' experiences*. Routledge.

Hollis, L. P. (2021c). Is bullying baked into the University? The organizational placement of human resources and its relationship with workplace bullying. In L. P. Hollis (Ed.), *Human resource perspectives on workplace bullying in higher education: Understanding vulnerable employees' experiences*. Routledge.

Hollis, L. P. (2021d). Bullied about? Lawyer up! When workplace bullying evolves into legal complaints. *Lawyer up*. In L. P. Hollis (Ed.), *Human resource perspectives on workplace bullying in higher education: Understanding vulnerable employees' experiences*. Routledge.

Hollis, L. P. (2021e). Ombudsmen as potential peacemakers with workplace bullying in higher education. In L. P. Hollis (Ed.), *Human resource perspectives on workplace bullying in higher education: Understanding vulnerable employees' experiences*. Routledge.

Hollis, L. P., & Yamada, D. C. (2021). *Human resource perspectives on workplace bullying in higher education: Understanding vulnerable employees' experiences*. Routledge.

Krippendorff, K. (2009). *The content analysis reader*. Sage.

Lewis, D., & Rayner, C. (2002). Bullying and human resource management: A wolf in sheep's clothing? In *Bullying and emotional abuse in the workplace* (pp. 388–400). CRC Press.

Manning, K. (2017). *Organizational theory in higher education*. Routledge.

Northouse, P. G. (2021). *Leadership: Theory and practice*. Sage Publications.

Oncu, M., Kim, N., & Faith, M. S. (2015). Statistical power as a function of Cronbach alpha of instrument questionnaire items. *BMC Medical Research Methodology, 15*(1), 1–9.

Weber, M., Gerth, H. H., & Mills, C. W. (1946). *From Max Weber: Essays in sociology*. Oxford University Press.

CHAPTER 8

Affirming the Impact of Faculty Mentoring in Context of Workplace Bullying (2021)

Abstract Often academics find themselves in a panic dealing with workplace bullying. Issues about stress and anxiety are often reported in the open-ended survey comments, which are saturated with respondents' hurt and frustration. Further, those in the weaker positions, such as graduate students, post-doctoral colleagues, and assistant professors without tenure often develop strategies to cope with the very people who bully them. To find a solution, I pondered if strong mentorship helps junior faculty assuage the impact of bullying. The sample for this study was $n = 128$ non-tenured assistant professors. Using family systems theory [Chambers, *Australian and New Zealand Journal of Family Therapy, 30*(4), 235–246 (2009); Hooper, et al., *Contemporary Family Therapy, 34*, 29–43 (2012)], I created a multiple regression study with one dependent variable and five independent variables. The findings revealed that the mentor's knowledge was a statistically significant variable to mitigate perceptions of bullying. Hence, this chapter will review how to develop specific variables in instruments for predictive analysis. The Cronbach's Alpha process is presented step-by-step, and the chapter continues with the dissemination procedures and the findings; then the actual instrument is presented. The chapter also discusses the solo-authored book of which this data is a part.

Keywords Mentoring • Workplace bullying • Junior faculty • Cronbach Alpha

© The Author(s), under exclusive license to Springer Nature Switzerland AG 2024
L. P. Hollis, *Instrumental Social Justice in Higher Education*,
https://doi.org/10.1007/978-3-031-49289-1_8

101

Inspiration/Motivation for Study

While I had been in higher education for over 30 years at the time of this writing, I chose an administrative route early in my career before seeking a tenure-track faculty position. In my mid-40s, I was older than the average newly minted junior faculty member but had the experience of a seasoned administrator. Therefore, I knew firsthand the importance of proper communication, clear evaluations processes, and consistent mentoring Hence, I found the family systems theories applicable (Chambers, 2009; Hooper et al., 2012). Anyone who accepts a new position benefits from proper coaching and mentoring to learn the new job functions, institutional colleagues, and the political backdrop. Based on their study of 243 employees, Van Vianen et al. (2018) used a survey which they validated with Cronbach's Alpha = 0.86. Through survey research, Van Vianen et al. (2018) examined mentoring, motivation, job satisfaction, faculty, and intention to stay. They found that strong mentoring was directly related to career promotability and to an employee's intention to stay. Another study considered how mentoring diminishes an employee's perception of career stagnation (Kao et al., 2022). Foster and Hill (2019) also lauded the positive impact of mentoring in their study of 82 doctoral nursing students. Those with strong mentoring relationships had greater career satisfaction after they earned their degrees; further, they had stronger decision-making skills (Foster & Hill, 2019).

Additionally, those with diminished power in an organizational system are more likely to face bullying (Hollis, 2015). Junior faculty, post-doctoral students, and graduate students, along with underrepresented minorities, are the personnel most vulnerable to workplace bullying, with research on 257 respondents confirming that 63% of junior faculty are bullied (Hollis, 2017). As a result, 32% of this sample intended to leave higher education (Hollis, 2017). In this context, Haines and Popovich (2014) expressed that junior faculty require consistent and empathic mentoring during their striving for tenure. Hence, the career mentoring literature (Moake et al., 2023), and my focus on healthy work environments, motivated me to investigate if mentoring for vulnerable populations can help diminish the painful distraction that accompanies workplace bullying.

Design and Methods

Based on the literature about faculty mentoring and other studies on workplace bullying, I designed the original instrument used for this study. Often researchers have unique or innovative ideas which require an original instrument to facilitate the investigation. To recruit an appropriate sample for this study, in 2019 I visited several higher education websites to identify junior faculty, regardless of race, gender, or academic discipline. With their publicly available email addresses, I created a safe list used to distribute the link to the survey directly to faculty members' emails. A safe list can host hundreds of emails; for example, 500 emails can be loaded into a safe list and named such as facultymentoring@state.edu. The safe list approach minimizes the number of emails which are undeliverable through colleges' and universities' firewalls.

The central research question was:

RQ1: What aspects of Faculty Mentoring—the mentor's time spent with a mentee (IV1), mentor's knowledge as faculty (IV2), mentor's career support (IV3), mentor's impact on mentee's productivity (IV4), and mentor's counsel of personal matters (IV5)—and the intensity of workplace bullying that junior faculty perceive?

H1: There is an inverse relationship between the aspects of Faculty Mentoring—the mentor's time spent with a mentee (IV1), mentor's knowledge as faculty (IV2), mentor's career support (IV3), mentor's impact—and the intensity of workplace bullying that junior faculty perceive.

The study examined five independent variables in a multiple regression. Each variable is the result of a composite score. For instance, to develop independent variable 1 (Time Spent IV1), four questions gathered these data; each question was in Likert-scale style, resulting in the highest possible composite score of 20. The same process was implemented for each variable, which all resulted from a composite score.

1. Time Spent (IV1): This variable included the time in years of mentoring, proximity to the mentor, and the mentee's satisfaction with the time spent.
2. Personal Matters (IV2): This variable considered personal support such as the empathy from a mentor, a mentor's sense of humor, the overall career advice, and the mentor's ability to relieve stress.
3. Knowledge (IV3): This variable measured the mentor's academic knowledge, the mentee's specific research area, knowledge of faculty experiences, and the mentee's satisfaction with the mentor's knowledge.

4. Productivity (IV4): This variable is based on writing and conferencing activities with the mentor and on the mentee's increased productivity because of the mentor.
5. Career Support (IV5): This variable considered the friendship between mentor and mentee by analyzing if the mentee shared personal family problems, work problems, and personal perspectives regarding career advancement.
6. Workplace Bullying (DV1): This dependent variable included the perceived intensity of the bullying, the duration in years of bullying, if bullying hurt research, service, and teaching, and if bullying increased anxiety, compromised health, and hurt personal life and career trajectory.

Researchers can enjoy an intellectual latitude by developing original surveys. In the past 20–25 years, researchers have started to examine workplace bullying, with a few studying the phenomenon in the higher education context. Further, unique work dynamics for higher education faculty include subjective tenure cycles, promotion reviews, class evaluations, and a subjective milieu of politics and favoritism. Consequently, any researcher examining the empirical relationship between a newly recognized problem of workplace bullying and a common activity of faculty mentoring potentially needs to create an original instrument. Creativity in research yields groundbreaking knowledge derived from "seemingly incongruous factors" (Fairchild, 2017, p. 2). Artists and academics can pursue more interesting productivity through the mash-up. "The classic 'mash-up' is a striking aural form. It might confront the listener with Destiny's Child jamming or perhaps we might hear Public Enemy meeting up seamlessly with Herb Alpert" (Fairchild, 2017, p. 1). Other fields such as medicine (Balci et al., 2021) and law (Bedi, 2016) also bring together unlikely elements to create solutions. Hence, I suggest a "mash-up" thinking that is putting two ideas together to form an innovative analysis. With such creativity often comes the need to develop an original statement in social science research.

DECISION ON SAMPLE/POPULATION

My motivation for studying junior faculty is twofold. First, since the 1970s, colleges and universities have shifted their reliance to adjunct and contingent faculty (Hollis, 2015; House Committee, 2014; Kezar &

Maxey, 2013). The shift away from tenured faculty is associated with the mercurial economic environment. During recessions, employers strive to avoid permanent financial commitments (Hollis, 2017). Instead, much like a department store that hires seasonal help during the high demand holiday times, when colleges and universities rely on adjuncts, they are more agile and responsive to the demand for another course or the lack of demand that leads to course cancellation.

Second, junior faculty were the ideal population for this study because they are the most likely to face bullying given their diminished power in higher education organizational structures. This population is also ideal because they are presumably the newest personnel in their department. Without tenure, the junior faculty population is arguably the most vulnerable. However, though they may face bullying, they have their terminal degree. They are early enough in their careers that they could leave for another institution or choose to completely leave the higher education sector.

In the higher education context, even the smartest junior faculty benefits from guidance. Each department has politics and personalities which inform what scholarship is appreciated and who teaches which classes. These departmental politics also inform tenure and promotion. Consequently, as Crisp and Cruz (2009) along with Portillo (2007) stated, junior faculty benefit from the insightful guidance senior faculty can provide. If needed, mentors who are not associated with that junior faculty member's home institutions can give advice about potential job searches.

DISSEMINATION CYCLE

Examining workplace bullying, junior faculty, and mentoring included engaging the sample at an advantageous time of the academic term. To avoid commencement, convocations, and final exam periods, I sent the survey to junior faculty in February through April. This gave me time to analyze the data for the annual American Education Research Associate Conference in the following year. I sent the survey to potential participants every two and a half weeks and completed the process after four disseminations.

CRONBACH'S ALPHA FOR INSTRUMENT

When writing a grant proposal or submitting a paper to a high-end journal, reviewers want to confirm that the data in the study are valid. Since the findings are directly related to the instrument's validity, researchers should take care to tabulate the level of internal consistency for the survey by employing Cronbach's Alpha (Oncu et al., 2015). This is because the Cronbach's Alpha evaluates if the scales in the instrument are closely related. Instruments with stronger statistical power yield more reliable and valid findings.

According to Cronbach (1951), a researcher can use an alpha coefficient method to validate Likert-scale questions; further, Oncu et al., (2015) confirmed that the Cronbach's Alpha process is appropriate for true-false questions. Therefore, assigning Likert-scale values to multiple choice questions and evaluating questions for yes/no outcomes was the process I used for applying Cronbach's Alpha to this instrument.

My validating the instrument included conducting a Cronbach's Alpha tabulation with Excel. Instrument analysis resulting in a Cronbach's Alpha at 0.65 or above is considered sufficient, as 0.65 rounds up to the required 0.7 for acceptable reliability (Bujang et al., 2018). The Cronbach's Alpha at 0.64 or below is not acceptable; if the Cronbach's Alpha coefficient is too low, this means the instrument is not valid and will not result in reliable findings. For example, an instrument with a Cronbach's Alpha of 0.47 would be very weak, and the resulting data would not be reliable. Conversely, an instrument that produced a Cronbach's Alpha of 0.88 would have strong validity and the resulting data would be considered reliable. In short, the closer the relationship among instrument questions, the stronger the instrument is as a whole. The closer to 1.0 for the Cronbach's Alpha variable, the more reliable the instrument is. The goal of the Cronbach's Alpha is to confirm that the instrument's results are valid and reliable. I used the following steps:

Step 1: Conduct a pilot test to gather at least 30 complete responses for the Cronbach's Alpha analysis. Researchers have noted a sample of 10 to 40 is required to conduct the Cronbach's Alpha (Bonett, 2002; Fleiss, 1986; Hertzog, 2008), yet the more respondents' answers included in the Cronbach's Alpha analysis, the more confident one can be in the Cronbach's Alpha tabulation; I relied upon answers from 45 respondents for this mentoring study. Create an Excel spreadsheet with the questions labeling the top columns and the respondents' answers in the rows. Be sure to have the data analysis tool pack included in Excel.

Step 2: For each completed respondent, insert the numeral answer for each question. In this instrument, 29 questions were analyzed. See Fig. 8.1 for how to create and populate the spreadsheet. The instrument's first 12 questions included the informed consent and collected demographic information such as gender, race, sexual orientation, and salary. Figure 8.1 only shows the Excel sheet for questions 13 through 20, but 70 respondents' answers are put into the spreadsheet.

Step 3: Calculate the variance in each question using the variance function: = VAR.S(B2:B71).

When Column B is analyzed, the variance = 0.3707. Similarly, when Column C is analyzed, the variance = 1.6739. This function should be applied to all columns, resulting in a variance answer for each. For this instrument, 29 variances were tabulated for each of the questions. See Fig. 8.1 for steps three through six to conduct a Cronbach's Alpha.

Step 4: Once the variance for each column is tabulated, the sum of these variances should be tabulated = VAR.S(71:AD71). The sum of variance of all 29 columns = 62.86. This is Σs^2_i.

Step 5: Tabulate the sum total for each respondent row. For example, the sum for questions 13 through 46 for Respondent 74 equals 113. The

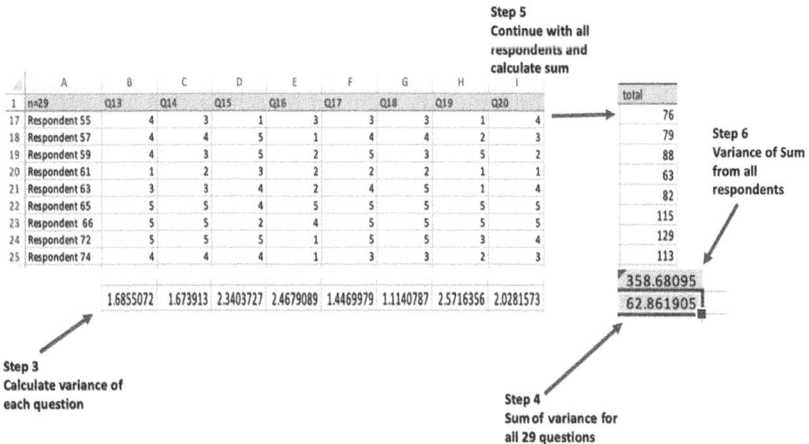

Fig. 8.1 Creating an Excel sheet for Cronbach's Alpha analysis

sum for Respondent 72 equals 129. Note, for example, Respondent 73 was skipped because the individual did not complete the survey.

Step 6: There should now be a final column for the sum of each respondent. Next, use the variance function to analyze the final sum column = VAR.S(AE2:AE71) with the resulting variable equaling 358.68. This is $s^2 y$.

Step 7: The Cronbach's Alpha formula is:

$$a = \frac{(n)}{(n-1)} * \frac{\left(s^2_y - \Sigma s^2_i\right)}{\left(s^2_y\right)}$$

N = the number of questions = 29
Therefore, for the Faculty Mentoring:

$$a = \frac{(29)}{(28)} * \frac{\left(358.68\{\text{variance of sum column}\} - 62.86\{\text{sum of variance}\}\right)}{\left(358.68 \text{ variance of sum column}\}\right)}$$

The Cronbach's Alpha for the Faculty Mentoring instrument = 0.86.

QUALITATIVE DATA

I designed this study for a multiple regression that examined five independent variables. The original instrument resulted in confirming the independent variable of mentor knowledge as statistically significant in helping junior faculty cope with bullying. By focusing on scholarship and productivity with a mentor, junior faculty could redirect their focus from the constant abuse and bullying. Additionally, even for a quantitative study, open-ended questions collect data that further support the quantitative analysis. This instrument presented this final open-ended question: *Do you have anything else you would like to share regarding your experience with workplace bullying?* Below, see three sample responses.

Respondent #174: After stewing over it for 3–4 years, I have finally decided to file an official complaint to HR. It is for my direct supervisor, chair of our department. Many others have experienced it as well, but everyone is afraid of retaliation. We are also at a [xxx] University so there is fear no one will believe us. I personally can't take it anymore and have gotten to the point that I either need to leave the University or file a complaint.

Respondent #219: Experienced extensive institutionalized bullying from a university President that trickled down through the administration to faculty. I left that university for my current position.

Respondent #304: This is a pervasive problem in my institution, and I believe it is exacerbated by restrictive laws in [state], where the only bullying or mobbing that is actionable is that perpetrated on protected classes (e.g., gender, ethnicity, etc.). This gives fairly free rein to those who would mistreat people who are part of otherwise privileged classes. My own academic career will likely end principally because of the awful experiences I have had re: bullying. As the doves are selected out, only hawks and their accomplices remain.

Qualitative data triangulate the findings from the respondents' perspective. Such data offer additional insight into the phenomena. Further, such information can support or inspire future research on the same topic.

RESULTING PUBLICATIONS

Often the data collected from survey research methods can be used for a variety of analyses. The demographic information is ripe for an analysis regarding a specific group. I could use the data to compare female junior faculty experiences and male junior faculty experiences and determine if men or women benefit most from faculty mentoring. Another study could examine the phenomenon regarding academic discipline. Workplace bullying may be more intense in the science fields as compared to the humanities. Nonetheless, I developed this study as a baseline examination of the impact of faculty mentoring on junior faculty who might be facing bullying.

From this baseline study, I incorporated these findings in a book chapter for a solo-authored book on human resources and workplace bullying. Often human resources personnel are either not trained or not charged by their leadership to address workplace bullying (Hollis, 2021). The data and findings could reinforce the need for more human resources intervention (Coyne et al., 2017; Harrington et al., 2012). Additional research could be conducted with this instrument to highlight differences along racial and gender lines.

Hollis, L. (2021). New Kid on the Block? Mentoring Junior Faculty and Dealing with Workplace Bullying. In Editor (Ed.), *Human resources perspectives on workplace bullying in higher education. Understanding Vulnerable employees' experiences.* Routledge.

AERA symposium. Faculty Development: Well-being, Workplace Bullying & Faculty Networks, University of Toronto, Canada. April 4–9, 2019.

REFLECTIVE QUESTIONS

The book and its chapters are meant to help new and seasoned researchers conduct Cronbach's Alpha for original instruments. Further, the instruments in this book can be used for research; of course, be sure to give the proper citation if one or any of the questions are used or modified for future research. The reflective questions in each chapter are meant to assist instructors in teaching Cronbach's Alpha processes.

1. What unique factor or dynamics in your academic discipline could benefit from a large sample quantitative study? In turn, how can Cronbach's Alpha help in the development of a new study?
2. This chapter discusses the "mash-up." What exactly is a "mash-up" and how can original instrument research assist in "mash-up" studies?
3. How can a literature review inform the researcher on which population to recruit?
4. Why is it important to know the statistical test (Chi-square, multiple regression, correlation, etc.) before developing the instrument?
5. What is a safe list and how does using the safe list strategy support instrument research?

APPENDIX: THE INSTRUMENT

Faculty Mentoring (2019)

How would you rate your satisfaction with your mentor? (Five (5) is the highest score–one (1) is the lowest score)

(If you have more than one mentor, answer regarding your PRIMARY mentor)

Very satisfied
Satisfied
Neutral
Somewhat satisfied
Not at all satisfied

How satisfied are you with the TIME SPENT with your mentor?
Very satisfied
Satisfied
Neutral
Somewhat satisfied
Not at all satisfied
How satisfied are you with the DISTANCE or PROXIMITY (miles) between you and your mentor?
Very satisfied
Satisfied
Neutral
Somewhat satisfied
Not at all satisfied
How many YEARS of the MENTORING relationship have you had with your mentor?
Five or more
Four
Three
Two
One
How satisfied are you with your mentor's knowledge?
Very satisfied
Satisfied
Neutral
Somewhat Satisfied
Not at all Satisfied
How satisfied are you with your mentor's applicable faculty experiences?
Very satisfied
Satisfied
Neutral
Somewhat satisfied
Not at all satisfied
How satisfied are you with your mentor's knowledge in YOUR SPECIFIC RESEARCH AREA?
Very satisfied
Satisfied
Neutral
Somewhat satisfied
Not at all satisfied

How effective is your mentor in helping you with stress?
Very helpful
Helpful
Neutral
Somewhat helpful
Not at all helpful
How effective is your mentor in providing CAREER ADVICE & ASSISTANCE?
Very helpful
Helpful
Neutral
Somewhat helpful
Not at all helpful
Is your mentor HUMOROUS in a way that helps with stress?
Very humorous
Humorous
Neutral
Somewhat humorous
Not at all humorous
Does your mentor have EMPATHY for you?
Very empathetic
Empathetic
Neutral
Somewhat empathetic
Not at all empathetic
Does your mentor help you manage workplace bullying?
Very much
Provides more than most
Neutral
Somewhat helpful
No help
Has your ACADEMIC PRODUCTIVITY increased because of your mentor?
Very much
Moderate increase
Neutral
Minimal increase
Not at all

How satisfied are you with your mentor in COLLABORATION (in writing)?
Very satisfied
Satisfied
Neutral
Somewhat satisfied
Not at all satisfied
How satisfied are you with your mentor in COLLABORATION (in conferencing)?
Very satisfied
Satisfied
Neutral
Somewhat satisfied
Not at all satisfied
How much do you tell your mentor about your personal problems (kids/spouse/partner/money)?
Very often
Sometimes
Neutral
Once in a while
Not at all
How much do you tell your mentor about OTHER PROFESSIONAL problems (job search, grants, CV review, peer reviewer issues, fellowships)?
Very often
Sometimes
Neutral
Once in a while
Not at all
How much do you tell your mentor about your TENURE PORTFOLIO problems (teaching, research, service)?
Very often
Sometimes
Neutral
Once in a while
Not at all
What is the intensity of workplace bullying for you?
Very significant
Significant

Average
Minor annoyance
Minimal annoyance
How many bullies are you subjected to?
Five or more
Four
Three
Two
One
What is the DURATION of workplace bullying for you?
Five or more years
Four years
Three years
Two years
One year or less
Has workplace bullying HURT YOUR RESEARCH?
Significantly hurt
Somewhat
Neutral
Minor hurt
Infrequent hurt
Has workplace bullying HURT YOUR SERVICE?
Significantly hurt
Somewhat
Neutral
Minor hurt
Infrequent hurt
Has workplace bullying HURT YOUR TEACHING?
Significantly hurt
Somewhat
Neutral
Minor hurt
Infrequent hurt
Has workplace bullying increased your ANXIETY/STRESS?
Significantly increased
Somewhat increased
Neutral
Minimal increase
Little or no increase

No stress/Anxiety
Has workplace bullying increased your INSOMNIA?
Significantly increased
Somewhat increased
Neutral
Minimal increase
Little or no increase
No insomnia
Has workplace bullying led to WEIGHT Swings (loss or gain)?
Significant swing in weight
Somewhat of a swing in weight
Neutral (up and down)
Minimal swing in weight
Little or no swing in weight
No weight swings
Has workplace bullying increased your ALCOHOL INTAKE?
Significantly increased
Somewhat increased
Neutral
Minimal increase
Little or no increase
No alcohol intake
Has workplace bullying led to PRESCRIPTIONS for SLEEP or STRESS?
Significantly increased
Somewhat increased
Neutral
Minimal increase
Little or no increase
No prescriptions
Has workplace bullying hurt your PERSONAL life (with kids, spouse, partner, friends, parents, etc.)?
Significantly hurt
Somewhat hurt
Neutral
Minimal hurt
Insignificant hurt
No hurt

Has workplace bullying contributed to you leaving a tenure-track position?
Significant contribution
Somewhat of contribution
Neutral
Minor contribution
Occasional contribution No contribution
Has the Bully broken or ignored laws, regulations procedures such as (but not limited to): Title VII civil rights laws, Title IX women's rights laws, University policy and regulations, Accreditation Standards?
Broken five (5) or more such laws or policies
Broken four (4) or more such laws or policies
Broken three (3) or more such laws or policies
Broken two (2) or more such laws or policies
Broken one (1) or more such laws or policies
No issues with such laws or policies

REFERENCES

Balci, C., Eşme, M., Sümer, F., Asil, S., Yavuz, B., Tuna, R., Özsürekci, C., Çalişkan, H., Ünsal, P., Ayçiçek, G. Ş., Halil, M., Cankurtaran, M., Doğu, B. B., & Şengül Ayçiçek, G. (2021). Long-term effect of masked hypertension management on cognitive functions in geriatric age: Geriatric MASked hypertension and cognition follow-up study (G-MASH-cog MONITOR). *Blood Pressure Monitoring*, *26*(4), 271–278. https://doi.org/10.1097/ MBP.0000000000000532

Bedi, M. (2016). The curious case of cell phone location data: Fourth Amendment doctrine mash-up. *Northwestern University Law Review*, *110*(2), 507–524.

Bonett, D. (2002). Sample size requirements for testing and estimating coefficient alpha. *Journal of Educational and Behavioral Statistics*, *27*(4), 335–340. https://doi.org/10.3102/10769986027004335

Bujang, M. A., Omar, E. D., & Baharum, N. A. (2018). A review on sample size determination for Cronbach's alpha test: A simple guide for researchers. *The Malaysian Journal of Medical Sciences: MJMS*, *25*(6), 85–99. https://doi. org/10.21315/mjms2018.25.6.9

Chambers, M. F. (2009). Nothing is as practical as a good theory: Bowen theory and the workplace—a personal application. *Australian and New Zealand Journal of Family Therapy*, *30*(4), 235–246.

Coyne, I., Farley, S., Axtell, C., Sprigg, C., Best, L., & Kwok, O. (2017). Understanding the relationship between experiencing workplace cyberbullying, employee mental strain and job satisfaction: A dysempowerment approach. *The International Journal of Human Resource Management, 28*(7), 945–972.

Crisp, G., & Cruz, I. (2009). Mentoring college students: A critical review of the literature between 1990 and 2007. *Research in Higher Education, 50*(6), 525–545.

Cronbach, L. J. (1951). Coefficient alpha and the internal structure of tests. *Psychometrika, 16*(3), 297–334.

Fairchild, C. (2017). The emergence and historical decay of the mash up. *Journal of Popular Music Studies, 29*(4). https://doi.org/10.1111/jpms.12246

Fleiss, J. L. (1986). *Design and analysis of clinical experiments.* Wiley.

Foster, T., & Hill, J. J. (2019). Mentoring and career satisfaction among emerging nurse scholars. *International Journal of Evidence Based Coaching & Mentoring, 17*(2).

Haines, S. L., & Popovich, N. G. (2014). Engaging external senior faculty members as Faculty mentors. *American Journal of Pharmaceutical Education, 78*(5), 1–6.

Harrington, S., Rayner, C., & Warren, S. (2012). Too hot to handle? Trust and human resource practitioners' implementation of anti-bullying policy. *Human Resource Management Journal, 22*(4), 392–408.

Hertzog, M. A. (2008). Considerations in determining sample size for pilot studies. *Research in Nursing & Health, 31*(2), 180–191.

Hollis, L. (2015). The significance of declining full-time faculty status for community college student retention and graduation: A correlational study with a Keynesian perspective. *International Journal of Humanities and Social Science, 5*(3), 1–7.

Hollis, L. P. (2017). This is why they leave you: Workplace bullying and insight to junior faculty departure. *British Journal of Education, 5*(10), 1–7.

Hollis, L. P. (2021). New kid on the block? Mentoring junior faculty and dealing with workplace bullying. In Hollis (Ed.), *Human resource perspectives on workplace bullying in higher education: Understanding vulnerable employees' experiences.* Routledge.

Hooper, L. M., Wright, V. H., & Burnham, J. J. (2012). Acculturating to the role of tenure-track assistant professor: A family systems approach to joining the academy. *Contemporary Family Therapy, 34*, 29–43.

House Committee on Education and Workforce Democratic Staff. (2014). *The just-in-time-professor: A staff report summarizing eForum responses on the working contingent faculty in higher education.* U.S. House of Representatives.

Kao, K.-Y., Hsu, H.-H., Lee, H.-T., Cheng, Y.-C., Dax, I., & Hsieh, M.-W. (2022). Career mentoring and job content plateaus: The roles of perceived organizational support and emotional exhaustion. *Journal of Career Development, 49*(2), 457–470. https://doi.org/10.1177/0894845320946399

Kezar, A., & Maxey, D. (2013). The changing academic workforce. *Trusteeship, 21*(3), 15–21.

Moake, T. R., Dougherty, T. W., & Dreher, G. F. (2023). Mentoring and career success: An examination of management aspirations and lengthy career interruptions. *Journal of Career Development, 50*(2), 482–498. https://doi.org/10.1177/08948453221113298

Oncu, M., Kim, N., & Faith, M. S. (2015). Statistical power as a function of Cronbach alpha of instrument questionnaire items. *BMC Medical Research Methodology, 15*(1), 1–9.

Portillo, S. (2007). Mentoring minority and female students: Recommendations for improving mentoring in public administration and public affairs programs. *Journal of Public Affairs Education, 13*(1), 103–113.

Van Vianen, A. E. M., Rosenauer, D., Homan, A. C., Horstmeier, C. A. L., & Voelpel, S. C. (2018). Career mentoring in context: A multilevel study on differentiated career mentoring and career mentoring climate. *Human Resource Management, 57*(2), 583–599. https://doi.org/10.1002/hrm.21879

CHAPTER 9

Verifying Women's Workplace Bullying Experiences at HBCUS and MSIs (2022)

Abstract Though most Historically Black Colleges and Universities (HBCUs) are four-year institutions, HBCUs are understudied when compared to Predominantly White Institutions (PWIs). Additionally, since workplace bullying is an understudied topic in higher education, this unfortunate workplace phenomenon receives even less attention in research about HBCUs and MSIs (minority serving institutions). To address the gap in the literature, I invited faculty from 45 HBCUs and MSIs in 15 states to participate in the study. With 65% of respondents identifying as women, I had an opportunity to conduct an analysis about workplace bullying and gender at HBCUs and MSIs. Theoretically, I applied Acker's [*Gender and Society, 2*, 139–158 (1990)] gendered organization theory. Arguably, women must still strive through patriarchal structures to advance their careers. Gendered organizational theory acknowledges that the most powerful positions in most organizations are held by men; hence, policies and practice reflect the male point of view.

Keywords HBCU workplace bullying • Gendered organization • Instrument development • Cronbach alpha

© The Author(s), under exclusive license to Springer Nature Switzerland AG 2024
L. P. Hollis, *Instrumental Social Justice in Higher Education*,
https://doi.org/10.1007/978-3-031-49289-1_9

Since their inception, many HBCUs have been the parallel educational structure for formerly enslaved people. In the early 1800s a few educational options were available for free Black men through Lincoln University and Cheyney University in Pennsylvania and Wilberforce in Ohio (Albritton, 2012). A majority of HBCUs were established in the 1860s, on the eve of the American Reconstruction period, dating 1865–1877 (McNally, 2006); during Reconstruction, approximately 12 Black men were elected to Congress (Foner, 1988). Though various historical figures such as Frederick Douglass and Elizabeth Cady Stanton rallied for Blacks and women to have the right to vote (Dudden, 2011), Black women did not formally have the confirmed right to vote nationally until the 1965 Voting Act, which granted all Americans the right to vote (Crowley, 2013).

As noted by Blackshear and Hollis (2021), Black women struggle to find emotionally and psychologically safe spaces in higher education. Presumably, an HBCU campus would provide more safety along racialized lines (Elliott et al., 2018); however, Black women can have a very different experience. Bonner noted that the sexism that Black women face creates a demoralizing experience, leaving many Black women vowing "never to work at another Black school" (Bonner, 2001, p. 178). Nonetheless, women maintain their commitment to the race by serving the Black students who attend HBCUs. While some Black women may not have had the respect of male counterparts, women at HBCUs remained committed to the mission of educating Black students (Moses, 1989).

Motivation for the Study

I once served as a tenured faculty member at an HBCU. In that experience, I witnessed firsthand how men and women leaders would demoralize women colleagues. Strong women who were committed to academic excellence and modeling such for students often were vilified by arrogant or insecure leadership who seemed only interested in their self-advancement. During my time there, I wondered if discriminatory animus against women was a department-specific issue or something more pervasive across HBCUs. My motivation was twofold. First, I recognized that educational researchers had not developed a study specifically about HBCUs, women, and workplace bullying. Additionally, when I was an HBCU educational researcher, I repeatedly watched, and experienced at times, how some women leaders consistently and aggressively sought to destroy other women. By surveying 45 HBCUs and MSIs, I could determine if sexist animus was only at my former institution or an issue for many HBCUs and MSIs. Theoretically, I found Ackers (1990) gendered organizational theory to be appropriate.

Design and Methods

I have found mixed methods research to be more rigorous than qualitative or quantitative methods alone. The statistics from a quantitative method can offer predictive findings ripe for decisions and policy development. Simultaneously, qualitative research gives voice to the disenfranchised (Hoover et al., 2018); in turn, researchers can uncover how and why occurrences manifest. My goal was to analyze the complex intersection of historical sexism and racism, couched in an educational structure often designed for formerly enslaved people and initially operated by white men. Within this milieu, understanding women's experiences at HBCUs and MSIs reasonably needed the more complex mixed methods research approach.

Houghton and Paniagua-Avila (2023) confirmed that mixed methods enhance epistemology and understanding of "causal structures" beyond statistical models (p. 1). Multiple data sources advance triangulation of the respondents' perspective with the statistical data. Consequently, when cultural elements are better understood in tandem with the statistical findings which confirm measurable patterns, researchers uncover a more comprehensive and empirically supported perspective.

The survey for this study gathered respondents' comments about their experiences working at an HBCU or MSI. As no other study has examined workplace bullying, women, and HBCUs/MSIs, I needed to develop an original instrument. With the statistical tests of chi-square and multiple regression in mind, I developed the survey for dissemination in fall 2020.

Decision on Sample/Population

The sample for this study came from 45 HBCUs and MSIs across 15 states. Given that the stated population was HBCU and MSI faculty, I recruited potential participants by visiting various college and university websites to gather the publicly available faculty emails. Gathering emails in this manner allowed me to purposely recruit faculty across all academic disciplines.

DISSEMINATION CYCLE

I relied on a dissemination cycle similar to previous workplace bullying research that I had conducted over the years. For potential respondents to complete the study, they should get an invitation and then three reminders every seven to ten days to complete the study. When I utilized this process, the most considerable boost to participation came in the second reminder. After the studies in 2012 through 2017, I modified the data collection process. Previously, I used software to distribute invitations en masse to 3000 emails through AOL, MSN, or Yahoo. The ".com" designation resulted in emailed invitations being blocked by various firewalls at colleges and universities, which led to invitations being undeliverable. Currently, I have learned to ask my home institution's IT department to create a safe list of all emails. This means that instead of a series of single emails being sent at once and then being flagged as spam, most emails are part of a safe list. The Gmail-based safe list enables me to send bulk emails without those invitations being caught in firewalls.

CRONBACH'S ALPHA FOR INSTRUMENT

When writing a grant proposal or submitting a paper to a high-end journal, reviewers want to confirm that the data in the study are valid. Since the findings are directly related to the instrument's validity, researchers should take care to tabulate the level of internal consistency for the survey by employing Cronbach's Alpha (Oncu et al., 2015). This is because the Cronbach's Alpha evaluates if the scales in the instrument are closely related. Instruments with stronger statistical power yield more reliable and valid findings. According to Cronbach (1951), a researcher can use an alpha coefficient method to validate Likert-scale questions; further, Oncu et al., (1995) confirmed that the Cronbach's Alpha process is appropriate for true-false questions. Therefore, assigning Likert-scale values to multiple choice questions and evaluating questions for yes/no outcomes was the process I used for applying Cronbach's Alpha to this instrument.

My validating the instrument included conducting a Cronbach's Alpha tabulation with Excel. Instrument analysis resulting in a Cronbach's Alpha at 0.65 or above is considered sufficient, as 0.65 rounds up to the required 0.7 for acceptable reliability (Bujang, Omar, & Baharum, 2018). The Cronbach's Alpha at 0.64 or below is not acceptable; if the Cronbach's

Alpha coefficient is too low, this means the instrument is not valid and will not result in reliable findings. For example, an instrument with a Cronbach's Alpha of 0.47 would be very weak, and the resulting data would not be reliable. Conversely, an instrument that produced a Cronbach's Alpha of 0.88 would have strong validity and the resulting data would be considered reliable. In short, the closer the relationship among instrument questions, the stronger the instrument is as a whole. The closer to 1.0 for the Cronbach's Alpha variable, the more reliable the instrument is. The goal of the Cronbach's Alpha is to confirm that the instrument's results are valid and reliable. I used the following steps:

Step 1: Conduct a pilot test to gather complete responses for the Cronbach's Alpha analysis. Researchers have noted a sample of 10 to 40 is required to conduct the Cronbach's Alpha (Bonett, 2002; Fleiss, 1986; Hertzog, 2008), yet the more respondents' answers that are included in the Cronbach's Alpha analysis, the more confident one can be in the Cronbach's Alpha tabulation. I relied upon answers from 50 respondents for this HBCU study. Create an Excel spreadsheet with the questions labeling the top columns and the respondents' answers in the rows. Be sure to have the data analysis tool pack included in Excel.

Step 2: For each completed respondent, insert the numeral answer for each question. In this instrument, 19 questions were analyzed. See Fig. 9.1 for how to create and populate the spreadsheet. The instrument's first 12 questions included the informed consent and collected demographic information such as gender, race, sexual orientation, and salary. Figure 9.1 only shows the Excel sheet for questions 10 through 18, but 50 respondents' answers to 19 questions are put into the spreadsheet.

Step 3: Calculate the variance in each question using the variance function: =VAR.S(B2:B50).

When Column C was analyzed, the variance = 2.4166667. Similarly, when Column D was analyzed, the variance = 2.6062925. This function should be applied to all columns, resulting in a variance answer for each. For this instrument, 19 variances were tabulated for each of the questions. See Fig. 9.1 for steps three through six to conduct a Cronbach's Alpha.

Step 4: Once the variance for each column is tabulated, the sum of these variances should be tabulated = VAR.S(B51:T51). The sum of variance of all 19 columns = 62.3248299.

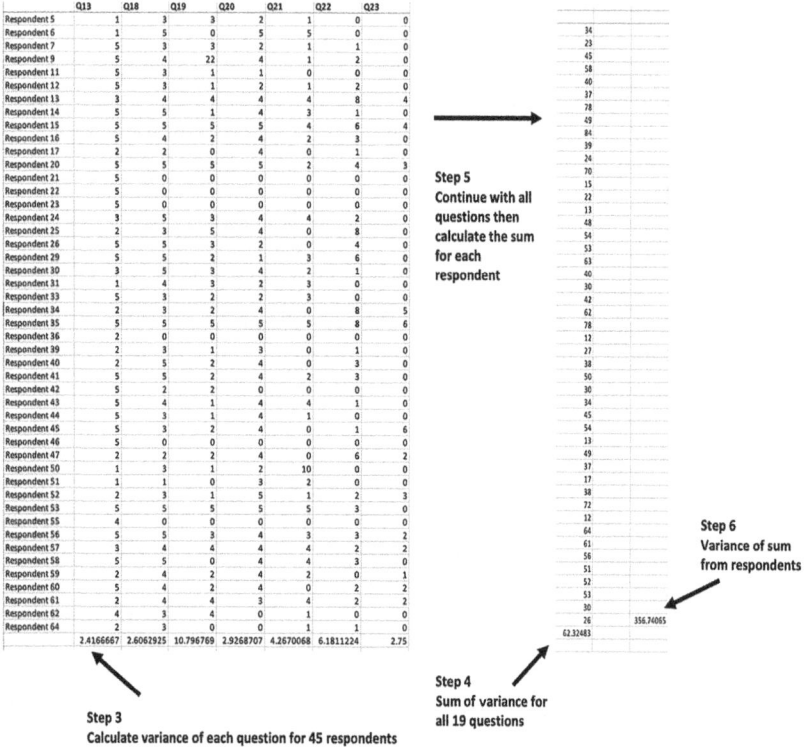

Fig. 9.1   Creating Excel sheet for Cronbach's Alpha analysis

Step 5: Tabulate the sum total for each respondent row. For example, the sum for questions 13 through 36 for Respondent 64 equals 26. The sum for Respondent 62 equals 30. Note, for example, Respondent 63 was skipped because this individual did not complete the survey.

Step 6: There should now be a final column for the sum of each respondent, represented here in column U. Next, use the variance function to analyze the final sum column =VAR.S(K2:K46), with the resulting variable equaling 356.74. This is s^2y.

Step 7: The Cronbach's Alpha formula is:

$$\alpha = \frac{(n)}{(n-1)} * \frac{\left(s^2_y - \Sigma s^2_i\right)}{\left(s^2_y\right)}$$

N = the number of questions = 19

$$a = \frac{(19)}{(18)} * \frac{\left(356.74\{\text{variance of sum column}\} - 62.32\{\text{sum of variance}\}\right)}{\left(356.74\{\text{variance of sum column}\}\right)}$$

The Cronbach's Alpha for the HBCU instrument = 0.87.

Publications

The results of this study led to a peer-reviewed article in the *Journal of Education*.

Hollis, L. P. (2022). In the room, but no seat at the table: Mixed methods analysis of HBCU women faculty and workplace bullying. *Journal of Education*, 2205742211023. https://doi.org/10.1177/0022057422 1102329

Also, I presented this data at the AERA National meeting in April 2022, in San Diego, California.

AERA Symposium: Exclusionary Tactics: A Multiple Regression Analysis of Women's Workplace Bullying Experiences at HBCUs. Organizer SIG: Critical Examination of Race, Ethnicity, Class, and Gender in Education, San Diego, California. April 22–25.

Reflective Questions

The book and its chapters are meant to help new and seasoned researchers conduct Cronbach's Alpha for original instruments. Further, the instruments in this book can be used for research; of course, be sure to give the proper citation if one or any of the questions are used or modified for future research. The reflective questions in each chapter are meant to assist instructors in teaching Cronbach's Alpha processes.

1. This chapter reflects on a data collection process that had a specific area, HBCUs and MSIs. As you consider your study, what compelling elements must you consider so you can recruit a proper sample?

2. To conduct this study specifically in HBCUs and MSIs, I needed to gather email addresses from public websites. Consider the population you might want to study. How can you get access to them so you can conduct your study?

3. What is the most difficult part of the Cronbach's Alpha process for you? Please identify the issue to discuss with your professor/instructor.

4. The demographic data allowed the researcher to create a comparative study focused on women. How can you use the demographic intake portion of the survey to create a similar analysis?

5. What statistical tests do you like best? Next, how can you create an instrument with the proper variable to support such an analysis?

APPENDIX: THE INSTRUMENT

Women's Workplace Bullying Experiences at HBCUS & MSIs (2022)

Does your campus have an explicit anti-bullying policy that specifically uses the term WORKPLACE BULLYING? (Pick one).

Yes, but no one follows it

No, and no one talks of creating a policy

Yes, it helps maintain peace

Yes, but policy is hard to find (not clear on website or in manual).

No, but we are talking about developing one

What is the intensity of workplace bullying for you at your MSI?

Very significant

Significant

Average

Minor annoyance

Minimal annoyance

How many bullies are you subjected to at your school? Five or more

Four

Three

Two

One

N/A

Has workplace bullying HURT YOUR JOB PERFORMANCE?

Significantly hurt
Somewhat
Neutral
Minor hurt Infrequent hurt
N/A
Has the Bully broken or ignored laws, regulations procedures such as (but not limited to): Title VII civil rights laws, Title IX women's rights laws, University policy and regulations, Accreditation Standards?
Broken five (5) or more such laws or policies
Broken four (4) such laws or policies
Broken three (3) such laws or policies
Broken two (2) such laws or policies
Broken one (1) such laws or policies
No issues with such laws or policies
How much time a week do you spend strategizing on the job to avoid bullying? 8 hours
7 hours
6 hours
5 hours
4 hours
3 hours
2 hours
1 hour
No time (please specify)
How many days a month do you miss work to avoid the bully?
6 or more
5 days
4 days
3 days
2 days
1 day
None
(Please specify)
What is the DURATION of workplace bullying for you?
Five or more years
Four years
Three years
Two years
One year or less

N/A

How much **time a week** do you spend supporting and/or commiserating with a colleague who is targeted by workplace bullying at your MSI?

8 hours or more

7 hours

6 hours

5 hours

4 hours

3 hours

2 hours

1 hours

No time

How much **time a week** do YOU RELY upon OR NEED another colleague to support you because YOU have been bullied at your MSI?

8 hours or more

7 hours

6 hours

5 hours

4 hours

3 hours

2 hours

1 hours

No time

What strategies do you use to avoid the bully?

(Check all that apply) Meetings off campus

Mid-day doctor appointments

Create childcare conflicts

Create elder care conflicts

Conferences off campus

Meetings away from your department (and the bully)

Late lunches

Leave work early

Arrive at work late

Work on weekends

Skip meetings with the bully N/A

Other (please specify)

Think of your career at MSIs. Have you left an MSI to avoid the toxic behavior or effect of a bully on staff?

Workplace bullying was more than 80% of reason I left an MSI

Workplace bullying was a majority of the reason leaving an MSI

Workplace bullying was part of the reason, but it was also a good move for my career. Workplace bullying was a minor reason for leaving an MSI

Workplace bullying was not the compelling reason, but a small factor for leaving an MSI

N/A

Think of your MSI. How likely are you to recommend your college or university to a friend for work?

I definitely WOULD NOT recommend a friend to work at an MSIs

I doubt I would recommend an MSI to a friend

A job is a job, if my friend needed a job so be it

It depends on the job if I would recommend a friend to work at an MSI

I definitely WOULD recommend a friend to work at an MSI

N/A

What behaviors have you engaged to deal with workplace bullying?

Increased intake of INSOMNIA MEDICINE to cope

Increased ALCOHOL use to cope

Increased intake of SEDATIVES (prescription or over the counter)

Experienced SUICIDAL ideation Other (please specify)

Increased use of MARIJUANA

Increased use of TOBACCO products (cigars, cigarettes)

N/A

For your next career move, will you consider an MSI?

I will never work for another MSI if I can help it.

I prefer NOT to work at another MSI.

A job is a job, MSI or not

I prefer working at an MSI, but would seek a healthy work environment.

Definitely, regardless of problems, I would seek another MSI

N/A

How much do you trust your MSI to treat you with respect and integrity?

I have NO TRUST at all

I minimally TRUST my MSI

I am neutral on the TRUST issue

I TRUST my MSI more than other places I have worked

I LOVE my MSI and definitely trust them

Do you feel valued at your MSI job?

Not at all

Somewhat

Neutral
Yes I feel very much valued
Yes I absolutely feel valued
Think of your MSI. How likely are you to recommend your college or
university to your child or other family to an MSI for college?
I definitely WOULD NOT recommend a child/family to attend an MSI
I doubt I would recommend a child/family to attend an MSI
School is school, if the financial package is good so be it
It depends on the major if I would recommend a child/family to an MSI
I definitely WOULD recommend a child/family to attend an MSI
N/A
Have your friends of family encouraged you to leave your MSI position?
Absolutely, they send me job announcements to help me leave and/or
really encourage me to leave
They regularly encourage me to leave
Neutral on this issue
They mention it from time to time
No they think I have a great job at my MSI

REFERENCES

Acker, J. (1990). Hierarchies, jobs, bodies: A theory of gendered organization. *Gender and Society, 2,* 139–158.

Albritton, T. (2012). Education our own: The historical legacy of HBCUs and their relevance for education a new generation of leaders. *The Urban Review, 44,* 311–331.

Blackshear, T., & Hollis, L. P. (2021). Despite the place, can't escape gender and race: Black women's faculty experiences at PWIs and HBCUs. *Taboo: The Journal of Culture and Education, 20*(1), 28–50.

Bonett, D. (2002). Sample size requirements for testing and estimating coefficient alpha. *Journal of Educational and Behavioral Statistics, 27*(4), 335–340. https://doi.org/10.3102/10769986027004335

Bonner, F. B. (2001). Addressing gender issues in the historically black college and university community: A challenge and call to action. *The Journal of Negro Education, 70*(3), 176–191. https://doi-org.ezaccess.libraries.psu.edu/10.2307/3211209

Bujang, M. A., Omar, E. D., & Baharum, N. A. (2018). A review on sample size determination for Cronbach's alpha test: A simple guide for researchers. *The Malaysian Journal of Medical Sciences: MJMS, 25*(6), 85–99. https://doi.org/10.21315/mjms2018.25.6.9

Crowley, R. (2013). 'The goddamndest, toughest voting rights bill': Critical Race Theory and the Voting Rights Act of 1965. *Race Ethnicity and Education, 16*(5), 696–724. https://doi.org/10.1080/13613324.2012.725037

Cronbach, L. J. (1951). Coefficient alpha and the internal structure of tests. *Psychometrika, 16*(3), 297–334.

Dudden, F. (2011). *Fighting changes: The struggle over woman suffrage and black suffrage in Reconstruction America.* Oxford University Press.

Elliott, K. C., Gregory, B. R., & de Gregory, C. A. (2018). "Yet with a steady beat": Advocating historically black colleges and Universities as black women in the age of trump's America. *Women, Gender, and Families of Color, 6*(1), 12–17. https://doi-org.ezaccess.libraries.psu.edu/10.5406/womgenfamcol. 6.1.0012

Fleiss, J. I. (1986). *The design and analysis of clinical experiments.* New York Wiley.

Foner, E. (1988). *Reconstruction, America's unfinished revolution 1863–1877.* Harper Collins.

Hertzog, M. A. (2008). Considerations in determining sample size for pilot studies. *Research in Nursing & Health, 31*(2), 180–191.

Hollis, L. P. (2022). In the room, but no seat at the table: Mixed methods analysis of HBCU women faculty and workplace bullying. *Journal of Education, 2205742211023.* https://doi.org/10.1177/00220574221102329

Hoover, S. M., Strapp, C. M., Ito, A., Foster, K., & Roth, K. (2018). Teaching qualitative research interviewer skills: A developmental framework for social justice psychological research teams. *Qualitative Psychology (Washington, DC), 5*(2), 300–318. https://doi.org/10.1037/qup0000101

Houghton, L., & Paniagua-Avila, A. (2023). Why and how epidemiologists should use mixed methods. *Epidemiology, 34*(2), 175–185. https://doi.org/10.1097/EDE.0000000000001565

McNally, M. J. (2006). Reconstruction and Parish Life in Charleston, South Carolina, 1865–1877: A Pastor's Perspective. *American Catholic Studies, 117*(1), 45–67. http://www.jstor.org/stable/44194975

Moses, Y. T. (1989). Black women and academe issues and strategies. In *Project on the status and education of women* (pp. 1–28). Association of American Colleges.

Oncu, M., Kim, N., & Faith, M. S. (2015). Statistical power as a function of Cronbach alpha of instrument questionnaire items. *BMC Medical Research Methodology, 15*(1), 1–9.

CHAPTER 10

Running with the Bulls: The Validated Concerns of Black Women Coaches' Workplace Bullying Experiences (2022)

Abstract An understudied topic in higher education is Black women coaches in intercollegiate athletics. Black women face an intersectional problem of being a racial minority and a woman in the white male-dominated area of college athletics. Therefore, I designed this instrument to query Black women coaches from Division I and Division II athletics to learn if they face workplace bullying and how such experiences may affect their career trajectory. Primarily, Black women coach women's basketball, women's track and field, and volleyball. In addition to the quantitative aspect of the chapter, the open-ended comments resulted in qualitative data that gave a more complete picture of Black women coaches' experiences. Using Pratto et al.'s [*Journal of Cross-Cultural Psychology, 31*(3), 369–409 (2000)] social dominance theory, I analyzed the sample of $n = 106$. The Cronbach's Alpha process is presented step-by-step. The chapter continues with the dissemination procedures and the findings, inclusive of the qualitative themes developed from the open-ended questions. Then the actual instrument is presented. This instrument provides another example of how the data from open-ended questions produce qualitative themes which support the quantitative data. The chapter concludes by describing the solo-authored book and conference presentations.

Keywords Black women • College athletics • NCAA • Intersectionality • Coaching • Workplace bullying

Inspiration/Motivation for Study

As Ofoegbu (2022) confirmed, Black women in athletics remain misunderstood; Carter-Francique (2018) reported through the 2016 *Racial and Gender Report Card* for college sports that Black women are only 3.1% of women's college sport head coaches (TIDES, n.d.). Larsen et al. (2019) reported even more unfortunate numbers by stating Blacks are only one percent of head coaches. Though Black women have increased their numbers in college sports participation since the inception of Title IX (Hollis, 2023), the same proportions are not evident in college athletic administration. Regardless of the topic, researchers need a working understanding about the context under investigation. If one were to study environmental issues in the southwestern United States, they should be conversant with the area, its environmental history, and potential changes. The same argument applies to studying human beings; the researcher should know the context. For this study on athletics, I am a researcher who played on a state championship high school volleyball team and lettered in college varsity volleyball. I also worked in athletics administration for nine years and understand firsthand the dynamics facing women in athletics. Even if a researcher has direct experience with a topic, the literature review is critical in developing a study that creates new knowledge and provides groundwork for additional future studies. Having a background in an area is not enough to inform survey development; an in-depth literature review should always be part of the process.

Though American higher education might occasionally focus on diversity and inclusion efforts, studies on Black women coaches in Division I and Division II athletics appear infrequently. A recent search on Google Scholar resulted in a few studies on Black women coaches stretching back to the mid-1980s. With these dated studies reported on the first page of the Google Scholar results, one can infer that Black women coaches as the central focus in empirical research has not occurred with the same frequency as athletics research in general. Given my interest and background in athletics, and my research agenda on workplace bullying, I was motivated to examine Black women coaches and workplace bullying experiences.

Decision on Sample/Population

I recruited Black women coaches for this study by first compiling the list of Division I and Division II athletics programs. With that list, I went to each athletic department to acquire the email addresses of Black women head coaches, associate coaches, assistant coaches, and coordinators. To conduct a valid statical analysis, I needed at least 100 responses. To create a sample large enough, I took email addresses from Division I and Division II colleges and universities. Though the pictures on the website might indicate race, I also asked participants to confirm their race as one of the initial demographic questions. Consequently, 77% of respondents were from Division I programs and 23% were from Division II programs. Additionally, Black women tended to coach women's basketball, volleyball, track and field, and then other sports. The final sample was n = 106.

Design and Methods

The mixed methods design included the chi-square for the statistical analysis and the qualitative content analysis for the qualitative portion. The data were analyzed concurrently. Instead of the quantitative findings informing the qualitative questions, or the qualitative themes informing the quantitative intake, the findings from both methods informed the final results. The instrument gathered data for a chi-square analysis and a content analysis. The central research questions were:

RQ1: What is the difference in the racialized/gendered expectations to comply with mainstream appearance between Division I program and Division II program?
H1: Black women coaches and personnel face more pressure at the Division I level when compared to the Division II level.
RQ2: How do Black women coaches perceive their acceptance in their respective sports programs?

To analyze the open-ended comments, I used Krippendorff' procedures for qualitative content analysis (1989). The analytical steps include reducing the data by highlighting repetition in the remarks. For example, a common response from this sample was how their passion for their sport was misinterpreted. Once I identified common phrases, I used open coding and then cluster coding to identify themes (Creswell, 2014).

Data Collection Cycle

As a former athletics administrator, I understood the slow times in the athletics administration calendar. During in-season practice and recruiting season, coaches are less likely to address extraneous messages, such as invitations to surveys. Further, the basketball season specifically begins after Thanksgiving and continues through "March madness." With the athletic calendar in mind, I invited coaches to the study during an eight-week window from mid-September through mid-November in 2020. Also, while the historical moment did not seem to affect the data collection, please note that in fall 2020, the Covid-19 pandemic had interrupted educational delivery. I sent an initial invitation to coaches which also mentioned my athletics background. When potential participants perceive that the researcher is from the same background, in my experience, they seem to respond more quickly.

CRONBACH'S ALPHA FOR INSTRUMENT

When writing a grant proposal or submitting a paper to a high-end journal, reviewers want to confirm that the data in the study are valid. Since the findings are directly related to the instrument's validity, researchers should take care to tabulate the internal consistency for the survey by employing Cronbach's Alpha (Oncu et al., 2015). Cronbach's Alpha evaluates if the scales in the instrument are closely related; instruments with stronger statistical power yield more reliable and valid findings.

According to Cronbach (1951), a researcher can use an alpha coefficient method to validate Likert-scale questions; further, Oncu et al., (1995) confirmed that the Cronbach's Alpha process is appropriate for true-false questions. Therefore, assigning Likert-scale values to multiple choice questions and evaluating questions for yes/no outcomes was the process I used for applying Cronbach's Alpha to this instrument.

My validating the instrument included conducting a Cronbach's Alpha tabulation with Excel. Instrument analysis resulting in a Cronbach's Alpha at 0.65 or above is considered sufficient, as 0.65 rounds up to the required 0.7 for acceptable reliability (Bujang et al., 2018). The Cronbach's Alpha at 0.64 or below is not acceptable; if the Cronbach's Alpha coefficient is too low, this means the instrument is not valid and will not result in reliable findings. For example, an instrument with a Cronbach's Alpha of 0.47 would be very weak, and the resulting data would not be reliable. Conversely, an instrument that produced a Cronbach's Alpha of 0.88 would have strong validity, and the resulting data would be considered reliable. In short, the relationship among instrument questions can determine the strength of the instrument as a whole. The closer to 1.0 for the

Cronbach's Alpha variable, the more reliable the instrument is. The goal of the Cronbach's Alpha is to confirm that the instrument's results are valid and reliable. Please see the following steps:

Step 1: Conduct a pilot test to gather at least 20 complete responses for the Cronbach's Alpha analysis. Researchers have noted a sample of 10 to 40 is required to conduct the Cronbach's Alpha (Bonett, 2002; Fleiss, 1986; Hertzog, 2008). I relied upon answers from 50 respondents. Create an Excel spreadsheet with the questions labeling the top columns and the respondents' answers in the rows. Be sure to have the data analysis tool pack included in Excel.

Step 2: For each completed respondent, insert the numeral answer for each question. In this instrument, nine questions were analyzed. See Fig. 10.1 for how to create and populate the spreadsheet. The instrument's first 12 questions included the informed consent, which are not shown, and collected demographic information such as gender, race, sexual orientation, and salary. Figure 10.1 only shows the Excel sheet for questions 10 through 17, but 50 respondents' answers are entered into the spreadsheet.

Step 3: Calculate the variance in each question using the variance function: = VAR.S(B2:B71).

When Column B is analyzed, the variance = 1.4489. Similarly, when Column C is analyzed, the variance = 0.0723. The variance function should be applied to all columns, resulting in a variance answer for each. For this instrument, nine variances were tabulated for each of the questions. See Fig. 10.1 for steps three through six to conduct a Cronbach's Alpha.

Step 4: Once the variance for each column is tabulated, the variance of these sums should be tabulated = VAR.S(B73:AD73). The sum of variances of all nine columns = 17.86. This is Σs^2_i.

Step 5: Tabulate the sum total for each respondent row. For example, the sum for questions 9 through 18 for Respondent 52 equals 30. The sum for Respondent 52 equals 17. Note: If a respondent does not complete the survey, a researcher cannot use the respondent's answers.

Step 6: There should now be a final column for the sum of each respondent. Next, use the sum variance function to analyze the final sum column = VAR.S(K2:K50), with the resulting variable equaling 49.31. This is $s^2 y$.

Step 7: The Cronbach's Alpha formula is:

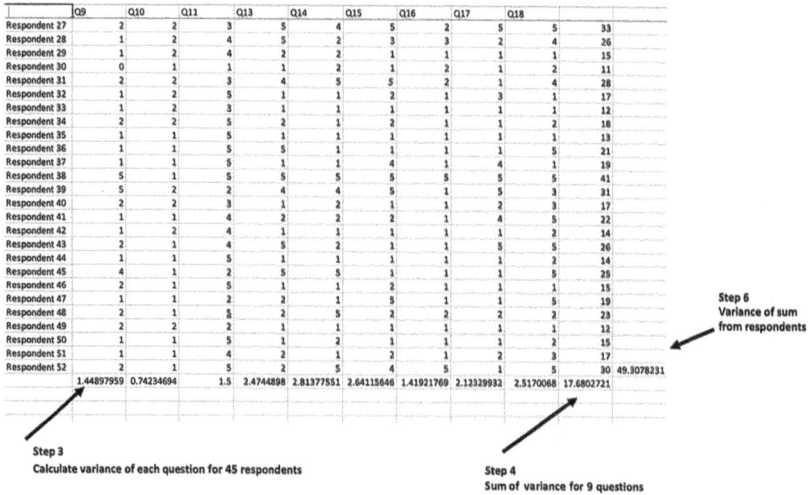

Fig. 10.1 Creating Excel sheet for Cronbach's Alpha analysis

$$\alpha = \frac{(n)}{(n-1)} * \frac{\left(s^2_{\,y} - \Sigma s^2_{\,i}\right)}{\left(s^2_{\,y}\right)}$$

N = the number of questions = 9
Therefore, for the Black women coaches:

$$a = \frac{(9)}{(8)} * \frac{\left(\left(49.31\{\text{variance of sum column}\} - 17.68\{\text{sum of variance}\}\right)\right)}{\left(49.31\{\text{variance of sum column}\}\right)}$$

The Cronbach's Alpha for the Black women coaches' instrument = 0.722.

*   *   *

RESULTING PUBLICATIONS

The findings from this study did not support a difference for Black women coaches and bullying regardless of their Division I or Division II status. Therefore, *H1 Black women coaches and personnel face more pressure at the Division I level when compared to the Division II level,* for the chi-square design is not accepted. Furthermore, the qualitative content analysis revealed interesting themes that researchers can consider for future study. This sample reported that being perceived as the "Angry Black Woman" interfered with respondents' ability to show passion and commitment for their teams in the same manner that men expressed their commitments. This theme aligns with Harris-Perry's (2011) study that confirmed that Black women are miscategorized as angry, even when their behaviors are similar to whites in the work environment. One respondent reported, "I was labeled as the angry Black girl, which silenced me" (Hollis, 2022). The instrument also allowed the researcher to reveal other emergent themes such as gender discrimination and the need for more Black women in college athletics. A salient theme also emerged, as some Black women felt lucky to have a good experience and not face pressure through sexual advances. Additionally, as this study included associate coaches and assistant coaches, some referred to their experience as being the "team mammy." They reported, "I strongly resent the implication that I am the 'team mom.'" Or "many times, I have been forced to confront African American student athletes about severe or minor problems because my White male head coach refused to handle their issues" (Hollis, 2022).

I published this study in a solo-authored book, *Black Women, Intersectionality, and Workplace Bullying: Intersecting Distress* (2022). As this book is part of a series with Routledge, I coordinated a book launch for the first three books in the series. The findings were also presented at an international conference for the Association of Black Sexologists and Clinicians, 7th Annual Round Table Conference in Montego Bay, Jamaica for a presentation titled "Team Mammy: Intersectionality, Black women and College Sports." Also, the findings from this study are slated for a free webinar style workshop. The goal will be to help Black women coaches network and also to empirically inform them of experiences their peers reported through the study.

As noted in other chapters, I recommend that researchers learn how to create truly new knowledge through mixed methods approaches. My research on Black women and coaches begins to address a gap in athletics research. Often, researchers focus on the student athlete experience, with emphasis on revenue sports (Bergman & Logan, 2020; Harrison et al., 2010; Hollis, 1998; Kahn, 2007; Sellers, 1992; Van Rheenen, 2013). Other studies may examine college athletics and leadership dynamics (Bower et al., 2015; Burton et al., 2009; Liu & Lin, 2012). However, though Black women are 9.3% of all student athletes, very few advance to coaching (Mathewson, 1995). In turn, the field also has a dearth of strategies and solutions to minimize gendered racism in athletics. When the body of research is small for any field, a researcher launching into that smaller research arena may not have a breadth of information that accompanies more popular or mainstream topic. Those researching less visible topics may need to develop their own instruments and practices to glean information from the proposed sample. Hence, a researcher should be able to create new investigations from these compelling yet understudied factors through original survey design and validation strategies.

REFLECTIVE QUESTIONS

The book and its chapters are meant to help new and seasoned researchers conduct Cronbach's Alpha for original instruments. Further, the instruments in this book can be used for research; of course, be sure to give the proper citation if one or any of the questions are used or modified for future research. In this context, reflective questions in each chapter are meant to assist instructors in teaching Cronbach's Alpha processes.

1. How can survey research assist in social justice initiatives? Please explain.
2. Why is original instrument research critical to understanding understudied populations?
3. Reflect on the population you wish to study. What must one consider about the timing in launching the study/inviting participants?
4. How many complete respondents does a researcher need to conduct a Cronbach's Alpha for an original instrument?
5. What subject knowledge do you have for your study? How should you learn more about the topic before designing the survey?

APPENDIX: THE INSTRUMENT

Black Women Coaches' Workplace Bullying Experiences: (2022)

Regardless of your true sexual orientation, have other professionals or players in athletics wrongly assumed you were gay?

Twice a year
Once a year
Every other year
Once in a while
Never
N/A

Have you ever faced sexual harassment, inappropriate touching, and/ or unwanted sexual comments while performing your job duties?

Twice a year
Once a year
Every other year
Occasionally throughout my career
Never

On a scale of one to five (five is the highest), please reply below to what best captures your thoughts about the following question:

If you were subjected to sexual harassment, unwelcome touching, and/ or unwanted sexual comments while performing your job duties, would you report it?

Absolutely
Probably
Not sure
Doubtful
Never

On a scale of 1 to 5 (five is the most or highest), do you feel pressure or an expectation to wear your hair a certain way? (Straight, long, draped over the shoulder and/or stylized custom cut).

At least twice an academic year
At least once an academic year
Every other year
Once in a while over the years
Never
Other (please specify)

On acale of 1 to 5 (five is the most or highest), do you feel pressure or an expectation to wear 'more feminine' clothes during competition (skirts, stockings, heels, dangle earrings, blouse with cleavage)?

At least twice an academic year
At least once an academic year
Every other year
Once in a while over the years
Never
Other (please specify)

On a Scale of 1 to 5 (five is the most or highest), do you feel pressure or an expectation to AVOID ethnic hair and clothes (braids, cornrows, ethnic print clothes)?

At least twice an academic year (5)
At least once an academic year (4)
Every other year (3)
Once in a while over the years (2) Never (1)
Other (please specify)

On a Scale of 1 to 5 (five is the most or highest), do you feel pressure or an expectation to wear demure and understated make-up?

At least twice an academic year
At least once an academic year
Every other year
Once in a while over the years
Never
Other (please specify)

On a Scale of 1 to 5 (five is the most or highest), do you feel pressure or an expectation to convince female players to be 'more lady-like.'

At least twice an academic year
At least once an academic year
Every other year
Once in a while over the years
Never
Other (please specify)

On a Scale of 1 to 5 (five is the most or highest), do you feel pressure or an expectation to conform to traditional norms about hair, clothes, and/or make-up when your image will be captured by the media (press, television, team photo, etc.)?

At least twice an academic year
At least once an academic year

Every other year
Once in a while
Never

References

Bergman, S. A., & Logan, T. D. (2020). Revenue per quality of college football recruit. *Journal of Sports Economics, 21*(6), 571–592.

Bonett, D. (2002). Sample size requirements for testing and estimating coefficient alpha. *Journal of Educational and Behavioral Statistics, 27*(4), 335–340. https://doi.org/10.3102/10769986027004335

Bower, G. G., Hums, M. A., & Grappendorf, H. (2015). Same story; different day: Greatest challenges of women working in intercollegiate athletic administration. *International Journal of Sport Management, Recreation & Tourism, 19*, 12–39.

Bujang, M. A., Omar, E. D., & Baharum, N. A. (2018). A review on sample size determination for Cronbach's alpha test: a simple guide for researchers. *The Malaysian Journal of Medical Sciences: MJMS, 25*(6), 85–99. https://doi.org/10.21315/mjms2018.25.6.9

Burton, L. J., Barr, C. A., Fink, J. S., & Bruening, J. E. (2009). "Think athletic director, think masculine?": Examination of the gender typing of managerial subroles within athletic administration positions. *Sex Roles, 61*, 416–426.

Carter-Francique, A. R. (2018). Is excellence inclusive? The benefits of fostering Black female college athlete's sense of belonging. *Journal of Higher Education Athletics & Innovation, 1*(3), 48–73. https://doi.org/10.15763/issn.2376-5267.2018.1.3

Creswell, J. (2014). *Research design: Qualitative, quantitative, and mixed methods approaches.* SAGE.

Cronbach, L. J. (1951). Coefficient alpha and the internal structure of tests. *Psychometrika, 16*(3), 297–334.

Fleiss, J. L. (1986). *Design and analysis of clinical experiments.* Wiley.

Harrison, C., Rasmussen, J., Connolly, C., Janson, N., Bukstein, S., & Parks, C. (2010). Diggin' deeper into the culture of revenue sports. *Journal for the Study of Sports and Athletes in Education, 4*(3), 325–332.

Harris-Perry, M. V. (2011). *Sister citizen: Shame, stereotypes, and Black women in America.* Yale University Press.

Hertzog, M. A. (2008). Considerations in determining sample size for pilot studies. *Research in Nursing & Health, 31*(2), 180–191.

Hollis, L. P. (1998). *Equal opportunity for student-athletes: Factors influencing student-athlete graduation rates in higher education.* Boston University.

Hollis, L. P. (2022). Track cleats and high heels: Black women coaches resisting social dominance in college sports. In *Black women, intersectionality and workplace bullying (ed. Hollis, L.P.) Intersecting Distress. Series: Women's Studies, Diversity Studies, Ethnic Studies, Black/Africana Studies, and Sociology.* Routledge.

Hollis, L. P. (2023). Title wave: Title IX and how compromised abortion rights can precipitate increased college drop-out rates. *Journal of Black Sexuality and Relationships.* (ed. Hollis, L. P.). *Special Issue on Black Women and Title IX, 10*(1), 1–8. https://doi.org/10.1353/bsr.2023.a910425

Kahn, L. M. (2007). Markets: Cartel behavior and amateurism in college sports. *Journal of Economic Perspectives, 21*(1), 209–226.

Krippendorff, K. (1989). Content analysis. In E. Barnouw, G. Gerbner, W. Schramm, T. L. Worth, & L. Gross (Eds.), *International encyclopedia of communication* (Vol. 1, pp. 403–407). Oxford University Press. http://respository.penn.edu

Larsen, L. K., Fisher, L., & Moret, L. (2019). The coach's journal: Experiences of Black female assistant coaches in NCAA Division I Women's basketball. *Coach, 3,* 632–658.

Liu, L. W., & Lin, C. H. (2012). Sport Management in collegiate athletic administration. *Procedia-Social and Behavioral Sciences, 40,* 364–367.

Mathewson, A. D. (1995). Black women, gender equity and the function at the junction. *Marquette Sports Law Journal, 6*(2), 239–266.

Ofoegbu, E. D. (2022). "Of Course I Was the Only Black Girl": Unpacking the academic experiences of black women student-athletes at PWIs. *Journal of Women and Gender in Higher Education, 15*(4), 396–414.

Oncu, M., Kim, N., & Faith, M. S. (2015). Statistical power as a function of Cronbach alpha of instrument questionnaire items. *BMC Medical Research Methodology, 15*(1), 1–9.

Pratto, F., Liu, J. H., Levin, S., Sidanius, J., Shih, M., Bachrach, H., & Hegarty, P. (2000). Social dominance orientation and the legitimization of inequality across cultures. *Journal of Cross-Cultural Psychology, 31*(3), 369–409.

Sellers, R. M. (1992). Racial differences in the predictors for academic achievement of student-athletes in Division I revenue producing sports. *Sociology of Sport Journal, 9*(1), 48–59.

TIDES. The Institute for Diversity and Ethics in Sport (n.d.). Reports. http://www.tidesport.org/reports.html

Van Rheenen, D. (2013). Exploitation in college sports: Race, revenue, and educational reward. *International Review for the Sociology of Sport, 48*(5), 550–571.

CHAPTER 11

Foundational Framing: A Brief Literature Review on Workplace Bullying Research Topics

Abstract Workplace bullying research, or any social justice research, should be couched in a thorough literature review. Researchers must gain insight into the academic field in which their study is situated by reading the most current literature and analyzing the findings of previous studies, allowing them to build upon that field of knowledge. When considering workplace bullying, one can identify many sub-topics such as race, gender, cost, and power. Hence, this brief literature review offers a sample of topics for workplace bullying researchers and demonstrates how social justice researchers can consider a range of vantage points under a single topic. When one considers the demographics, research environment, historical context, and past research findings, one can forge a path to new knowledge that further extends the field. By using the literature review as a foundation in instrument development, the researcher is better poised to discover new and groundbreaking findings. Note, typically a literature review should revolve around the keywords in a research question. Though still built on empirical research, this literature review incorporates the workplace bullying topics across eight book chapters, the topics in this literature represent a larger body of work rather than reflecting on a single research question. Nonetheless, any literature review should extend past simple reporting, but offer the reader an analysis of theories and data in a specific field.

L. P. Hollis, *Instrumental Social Justice in Higher Education*, https://doi.org/10.1007/978-3-031-49289-1_11

Keywords Workplace bullying • Literature review • Social justice

When people ask me to discuss workplace bullying, race, or gender issues in higher education, I respond with a request for more clarity in the question, as the generalist approach to inquiry does not reflect the complexity found in social justice work. Workplace bullying dovetails into several issues such as health, discrimination, cost, legal issues, and leadership, to name a few (Hollis, 2017a). Further, workplace behaviors are informed by race, gender, age, and other demographic information. In social justice work, additional issues such as intersectionality, work stress, ecosystems, organizational history, and a myriad of other issues inform the workspace. Consequently, a researcher can engage a variety of elements to create different perspectives and unique academic data collections to answer provocative questions.

To this point, an interesting metaphor to research is akin to when someone asks what kind of pizza they should order. Pizzas have different styles: thick crust, thin crust, pan pizza, cheese-filled crust, and Sicilian crust. Additionally, a consumer has multiple sauce options, including white sauce, marinara, or robust sauce. Further, the range of toppings allows for indefinite combinations such as plain cheese, four cheese, pepperoni, meat lovers, veggie lovers, and even ham/pineapple pizza. All of these combinations are available when someone asks, "What kind of pizza do you want?" Likewise, researchers have constant options when creating a research project. With this in mind, I developed a brief literature review of factors influencing inquiry and research development.

The pizza metaphor is like adopting research approaches for workplace bullying or any topic. A researcher must consider the topic within a specific issue. For example, a researcher studying Latinx, middle school students must decide if the sample would be boys, girls, gender-fluid students, or a mix of students with diverse gender orientations. The same researcher may consider the teachers and administrative staff who serve these students. The setting should also be taken into account; for example, the researcher could study students in the southwest, a specific state, or district. Each context will bring a different "flavor" or perspective to the study. Further, the researcher needs to decide if the students will be from a public school, a charter school, an online school, a private school, a Montessori setting, or even a mix of school types. One should consider if the data will be most helpful if it is solely quantitative. Perhaps data collected through open-ended survey questions or data from qualitative interviews can yield data that can support a mixed-methods study. Questions as a part of a qualitative interview or a survey can yield qualitative data for a more robust study. All these possibilities must be considered when designing a study and the most optimal survey instrument.

The pizza metaphor offers an interesting perspective on social justice research as well. Regarding workplace bullying, I could pursue gender issues, race issues, the cost, health and wellness concerns, and other aspects unnamed here. By engaging in a literature review, a researcher can better define what factors will inform the research questions and methods. The information below provides just a sample of issues examined in the context of workplace bullying research. By no means is this an exhaustive discussion, as it is meant to help researchers reflect on the many possibilities in this field.

HEALTH AND STRESS

Researchers from Scandinavian countries, Australia, France, and Canada consider workplace bullying a public health threat (Hollis, 2017a). The European Agency for Safety and Health at Work (EU-OSHA) and the World Health Organization (WHO) (EU-OSHA, 2009) have cautioned employees about workplace stress and the resulting health issues for over a decade. Specifically, harassment and bullying at work may result in insomnia (Nauman et al., 2019; Vartia, 2001) and anxiety disorders (Rodríguez-Muñoz et al., 2015). Additionally, such anxiety compromises workers' productivity (Wu et al., 2020) and contributes to depression (Lo Presti et al., 2019). As noted by Einarsen and Nielsen et al. (2015), "Workplace bullying and subsequent mental health problems [precipitate] anxiety and depression with a time lag of five years" (p. 131).

A more acute reaction to workplace bullying manifests in suicidal ideation. Ample evidence gathered through my previous investigations indicates that many individuals have considered taking their own lives to escape work abuse (Hollis, 2017b, 2019a, 2019b, 2022). Findings pertaining to different countries also consistently show that workplace bullying is linked to self-harming behaviors. For example, Nielsen et al. (2015) found that "Workplace bullying may be a precursor to suicidal ideation, whereas suicidal ideation seems to have no impact on subsequent risk of being bullied" (p. 105). In a study of 98,330 participants, Conway et al. (2022) confirmed that workplace bullying is associated with suicide, a finding that was subsequently corroborated by Lu et al. (2023).

Hanson et al. (2023) began their study with the premise that the association between workplace bullying and suicide is unclear. Nonetheless, their results confirmed that those who had weekly exposure to workplace bullying were at a higher risk of suicide. In addition, male participants were more likely to pursue suicide as a result of workplace bullying.

The body and brain are not built to withstand constant stress. Counseling can provide relief for those plagued by stressfully abusive bully bosses. As Namie (2003) noted, the psychological terrorism that one faces on the job can be addressed to some extent through counseling. Under abusive work conditions, an employee can be subject to a barrage of maltreatment that reasonably produces cognitive confusion (Finkelstein et al., 2009). Good people can make very bad decisions when they are inundated with stress; therefore, a culturally competent psychologist can help a patient sort through reactive and emotional decisions to make sound decisions while withstanding stressful abuse. Stated otherwise, such counseling should be offered by a psychologist or psychiatrist who understands the patient's background, demographics, and positionality.

A trained psychologist can administer eye movement desensitization and reprocessing (EMDR). "In 1989, EMDR was introduced to help trauma patients. Eye movement desensitization and reprocessing (EMDR) is an empirically validated psychotherapy approach that medical personnel can employ to treat the sequelae of psychological trauma and other negative life experiences" (Hollis, 2023, p. 9; Shapiro, 2014, p. 71). Foa and Kozak (1986) claim the patient must reactivate and then restructure traumatic events with new information (Rothbaum et al., 2005). Such noninvasive treatment uses eye movement to reposition trauma in the brain by activating a recuperative cognitive process akin to REM (rapid eye movement) sleep (Stickgold, 2002).

Bullied by Race and Gender, a Historical Perspective

Literature reviews often present some historical context for the topic being analyzed. Hence, I offer this brief historical perspective on power, race, and gender. Workplace bullying manifests when those in power exploit a power differential between them and less powerful colleagues, which may result in employees facing mistreatment (Laloo et al., 2019). Though a variety of workplace bullying definitions inform the field, most include common terms such as "systematic," "intimidation," "fear," "distress," "harm," and "power" (Houghton et al., 2021). Collective power can even be used for staff members to bully upward in the organizational chart. Regardless of the direction of the aggression—top-down, peer-to-peer, or mobbing upward—a power imbalance fuels the aggression (Patterson et al., 2018). Still, throughout history, power differentials have often involved race, wealth, class, and gender.

For instance, many scholars know the phrase, "the sun never sets on the British Empire." Additionally, the French, Spanish, and Portuguese have colonized Black and brown people around the globe for centuries. The colonists' language and customs were adopted by those local communities in an attempt to minimize imperialistic intrusion and abuse (Earle, 2010; Keesling, 1989). The United States used similar strategies when removing indigenous people from their ancestral lands across North America. Under President Polk, the Mexican-American War of 1846-1848 led to the United States annexing a large part of Mexico, and these territories later became California, Texas, New Mexico, Arizona, Utah, Washington, and Oregon. With Christian "justice" as the undergirding philosophy, the United States waged "one of the most unjust [wars] ever waged by a stronger nation against a weaker nation" (Grant, 1885, p. 53, 56; Pinheiro, 2022, p. 22). The action fulfilled President Polks' manifest destiny ideal that the young United States would expand to the Pacific Ocean (Eland, 2014). The United States history exhibits a quintessential example of how abuse of power, race, and class (resources) bullied Mexico out of its land.

Colonialism was driven by a more powerful country, flush with resources, that seeks to control less advantaged countries of color. Bonds and Inwood (2016) remark that colonialism was motivated by economic and militaristic goals. Within such systems, even colonized systems, women customarily, though not universally, held even less power, as gendered discourse was used to consistently advance the notion of women's inferiority (Mohanty, 1984; Ohene-Nyako, 2018).

In a historical macro ecosystem where a dominant culture seeks and sustains its domination, these underpinnings of power yield an environment where race, gender, and ethnicity distinctions signify who is disenfranchised and dispossessed. Within the aforementioned historical context in which women and people of color hold diminished power in their respective societies, the more contemporary workplace bullying phenomenon also involves power differentials along racial and gendered lines. For example, Fox and Stallworth (2005) found that Asians, Blacks, and Hispanics reported more workplace bullying than white employees in the same environment. Additionally, Wu et al. (2015) confirm that racial and ethnic bullying can yield a greater sensitivity to future mistreatment. Reasonably, I see how this finding is potentially applicable to women who also endure disproportionate rates of workplace bullying (Hollis, 2019a).

In 2019, Feijó et al. examined 51 research articles to consider the impact of race and gender on the prevalence of workplace bullying. Their analysis confirmed the prevalent view that women are more likely to endure workplace bullying. The authors also noted that younger people are more susceptible to bullying, as was previously confirmed by Hollis (2014) in a study involving workers under the age of 40. These results are attributed to the fact that both populations (those under 40 and women) traditionally lack in-depth organizational power. Feijó et al.'s (2019) analyses also reconfirmed that racial ethnicity was associated with the increased likelihood of being a victim of bullying.

Though one might be tempted to think of race and gender as intrinsic and genetic reasons why these populations encounter more bullying, the high rate of workplace bullying in these populations instead elucidates the powerlessness women and people of color experience at work. The circumstances in which women and people of color are more likely to be bullied are steeped in historical foundations that deny them power. The social structures and historical underpinnings, as noted through research on colonialism and imperialism, continue to hamper self-determination for these groups and instead leave them resisting maltreatment and aggression in their day-to-day work lives.

With workplace bullying recognized as an international problem, the American discussion on race and gender in the context of workplace bullying encounters a notably different issue. The 1964 Civil Rights laws prohibit harassment and discrimination on the basis of race, gender, color, ethnicity, disabilities, and other protected classes. A person from a protected class can access American laws about harassment through The Equal Employment Opportunity Commission (EEOC), which can then initiate investigations. However, if intragroup harassment occurs, such as woman-to-woman or Latinx-to-Latinx, the charge of discrimination based on protected class status can be challenged in courts. Yet, once someone files a good-faith complaint, whether or not the complaint is truly viable, that person is still protected from retaliation. After someone files such a good-faith complaint, if they are subjected to workplace bullying, they then have the grounds for a retaliation charge.

A few states have made mild attempts at addressing workplace bullying. California, Utah, Minnesota, Maryland, and Tennessee have laws that appear to provide more protection for employers than the powerless targets (Keashly & Hollis, 2022). In some cases, if an organization provides training, that organization escapes culpability if their managers bully employees, a stark difference to how Title VII laws hold employers responsible when their managers discriminate against employees. The strongest anti-workplace bullying law in the United States comes from Puerto Rico in the form of House Bill 306, passed in August 2020 (Santos & Colon-Acevdeo, 2020). The Puerto Rican law mirrors other American Civil Rights laws that hold employers responsible and allows complainants to come forward to combat workplace bullying as an actionable singular problem, not couched in retaliation categories or as an add-on to another charge.

Workplace Bullying Costs to Individuals and Institutions

Owing to my considerable experience as an administrator, I recognize that administrators often want to know the cost of something to inform their decisions. Just as administrators consider the return on investment for building facilities or hiring staff, they often look to the cost of interventions. Though workplace bullying researchers have continuously reported the expense incurred by the employer, Australian researchers, McTernan et al. (2013) estimated that depression related to workplace cost $AUD 8 billion per year and $AUD 693 million in preventable lost productivity. Hollis's (2015) study on American higher education estimates that the average bullied employee in higher education spends five weeks strategizing around and coping with a bully. Assuming a 40-hour week and the 4.24 hours on average this sample spent dealing with bullying, this is equivalent to a loss of $8834 per person for employees making an average salary of $80,000. Sabbath et al. (2018) found that those who did not experience workplace bullying spent $793 per year on mental health services, while those affected by bullying spent almost twice as much (at $1557 annually).

Turnover also impacts institutions, as the cost of replacing an employee is approximately 150% of their salary (Ruyle, 2012; Seaver, 2015). "United Kingdom (UK) based studies estimate that the annual cost of lost productivity (only) due to workplace bullying ranges from £1.5 billion to

£9.5 billion, while in Ireland in 2020, the lost productivity was estimated to be in the order of €239.3 million" (Ballard & Bozin, 2023; Cullinan et al., 2020, para. 47).

Hoel et al. (2020) cite other costs, such as the United Kingdom paying £709,000 to compensate soldiers who faced bullying. Hoel et al. (2020) also bring to the fore the case of Gerd Liv Valla, a leader of the Norwegian Trade Union Confederation, as once Gerd resigned, the Union spent close to two million US dollars on legal fees and investigations. Similar findings about the cost of workplace bullying were reported by Hollis (2012), who noted that a university lost close to $10 million when two women in an athletics department reported bullying. The school lost grants from the National Collegiate Athletic Association (NCAA), could not raise funds, paid hefty legal fees, and eventually lost its university president and athletic director, who allowed the abuse to span over four years (Hollis, 2012). In their review of 12 studies across five countries (Australia, Italy, Spain, the United Kingdom, and the United States) aiming to estimate the cost of workplace bullying, Hassard et al. (2018) wrote, "The annual cost of psychosocial workplace aggression varied substantially, ranging between $114.64 million and $35.9 billion" (p. 10).

Conclusion

Among the wide range of workplace bullying topics, health, race, gender, and cost are most widely researched. While most of these studies were conducted in the United States, an ample body of evidence also comes from Norway, Australia, and western Europe. Similarly, a researcher can also shuffle topics, environments, and demographics to craft innovative research.

Sage advice often suggests that one should start with the end in mind. To align with the opening metaphor, if one makes a pizza, one decides the ingredients and various options that can contribute to that meal. Just as one may choose vegetables, meats, and cheeses, the researcher must choose the topic, the variables, and the research environment. The literature review in this metaphor is like grocery shopping. The researcher is looking for the different ingredients and is determining which elements yield the best outcome. Not only for social justice research but research in general, a comprehensive literature review provides a critical foundation for survey development.

REFERENCES

Ballard, A., & Bozin, D. (2023). The true (financial) costs of workplace violence in Australia. *Alternative Law Journal, 48*(3), 191–196.

Bonds, A., & Inwood, J. (2016). Beyond white privilege: Geographies of white supremacy and settler colonialism. *Progress in Human Geography, 40*(6), 715–733. https://doi.org/10.1177/0309132515613166

Conway, P. M., Erlangsen, A., Grynderup, M. B., Clausen, T., Rugulies, R., Bjorner, J. B., Burr, H., Francioli, L., Garde, A. H., Hansen, Å. M., Hanson, L. M., Kirchheiner-Rasmussen, J., Kristensen, T. S., Mikkelsen, E. G., Stenager, E., Thorsen, S. V., Villadsen, E., & Høgh, A. (2022). Workplace bullying and risk of suicide and suicide attempts: A register-based prospective cohort study of 98 330 participants in Denmark. *Scandinavian Journal of Work, Environment & Health, 48*(6), 425–434. https://doi.org/10.5271/sjweh.4034

Cullinan, et al. (2020). The value of lost productivity from workplace bullying in Ireland. 70-*Occupational Medicine*, 251–258, 251, 255.

Earle, R. (2010). "If you eat their food…": Diets and bodies in early colonial Spanish America. *The American Historical Review, 115*(3), 688–713.

Einarsen, S., & Nielsen, M. B. (2015). Workplace bullying as an antecedent of mental health problems: A five-year prospective and representative study. *International Archives of Occupational and Environmental Health, 88*(2), 131–142.

Eland, I. (2014). *Recarving Rushmore: Ranking the presidents on peace, prosperity, and liberty*. Independent Institute.

European Agency for Safety and Health at Work (EU-OSHA). (2009). Workplace violence and harassment: A European Picture. https://osha.europa.eu/en/tools-and-publications/publications/reports/violenceharassment-TERO09010ENC

Feijó, F. R., Gräf, D. D., Pearce, N., & Fassa, A. G. (2019). Risk factors for workplace bullying: A systematic review. *International Journal of Environmental Research and Public Health, 16*(11), 1945. https://doi.org/10.3390/ijerph16111945

Finkelstein, S., Whitehead, J., & Campbell, A. (2009). *Think again: Why good leaders make bad decisions and how to keep it from happening to you*. Harvard Business Press.

Foa, E. B., & Kozak, M. J. (1986). Emotional processing of fear: Exposure to corrective information. *Psychological Bulletin, 99*, 20–35.

Fox, S., & Stallworth, L. E. (2005). Racial/ethnic bullying: Exploring links between bullying and racism in the US workplace. *Journal of Vocational Behavior, 66*(3), 438–456.

Grant, U. (1885). *Personal Memoirs of U.S. Grant 2 vols*. Charles S. Webster & Company.

Hanson, L. L. M., Pentti, J., Nordentoft, M., Xu, T., Rugulies, R., Madsen, I. E., et al. (2023). Association of workplace violence and bullying with later suicide risk: A multicohort study and meta-analysis of published data. *The Lancet Public Health, 8*(7), e494–e503.

Hassard, J., Teoh, K. R., Visockaite, G., Dewe, P., & Cox, T. (2018). The financial burden of psychosocial workplace aggression: A systematic review of cost-of-illness studies. *Work & Stress, 32*(1), 6–32.

Hoel, H., Cooper, C. L., & Einarsen, S. V. (2020). Organizational effects of workplace bullying. In *Bullying and harassment in the workplace* (pp. 209–234). CRC Press.

Hollis, L. P. (2012). *Bully in the Ivory Tower.* Patricia Berkly LLC Wilmington DE.

Hollis, L. P. (2014). Lambs to slaughter? Young people as the prospective target of workplace bullying in higher education. *Journal of Education and Human Development, 3*(4), 45–57.

Hollis, L. P. (2015). Bully university? The cost of workplace bullying and employee disengagement in American higher education. *Sage Open, 5*(2), 2158244015 5589997

Hollis, L. P. (2017a). Workplace Bullying II: A civilizational shortcoming examined in a comparative content analysis. *Comparative Civilizations Review, 77,* 90–104.

Hollis, L. P. (2017b). This is why they leave you: Workplace bullying and insight to junior faculty departure. *British Journal of Education, 5*(10), 1–7.

Hollis, L. P. (2019a). Her beleaguered libido: Black women's decreased desire and self-medicating reaction to workplace bullying. *Journal of Black Sexuality and Relationships, 6*(4), 99–114. https://doi.org/10.1353/bsr.2019.0028

Hollis, L. P. (2019b). Something to lose sleep over? Predictive analysis of black men's and white men's insomnia issues due to workplace bullying in higher education. *Journal of Black Sexuality and Relationships, 5*(4), 1–19. https://doi.org/10.1353/bsr.2019.0007

Hollis, L. P. (2022). In the room, but no seat at the table: Mixed methods analysis of HBCU women faculty and workplace bullying. *Journal of Education (Boston, Mass.),* 2205742211023. https://doi.org/10.1177/00220574221102329

Hollis, L. P. (2023). Spirit murdering and mobbing: Working strategies for underrepresented minority faculty survivors of academic workplace bullying. *Taboo, 21*(4), 6–20.

Houghton, J. D., Oxarart, R. A., Heames, J. T., et al. (2021). Leader power and agency-communion orientations as moderators of the effects of organizational characteristics on workplace bullying. *Employee Responsibilities and Rights Journal, 33,* 235–249. https://doi-org.ezaccess.libraries.psu.edu/10.1007/s10672-021-09379-x

Keashly, L., & Hollis, L. P. (2022). *Workplace bullying, not just another conflict.* De Gruyter Handbook of Organizational Conflict Management. Walter de Gruyter GmbH & Co KG.

Keesling, R. M. (1989). Creating the past: Custom and identity in the contemporary Pacific. *The Contemporary Pacific*, 19–42.

Laloo, E., Bakand, S., Hanley, N., Coman, R., & University of Wollongong, New South Wales, Australia. (2019). Reflections on group power differentials across one safety professional's career: In search of an optimal psychosocial safety climate. *International Practice Development Journal*, 9(2), 1–7. https://doi.org/10.19043/ipdj.92.009

Lo Presti, A., Pappone, P., & Landolfi, A. (2019). The associations between workplace bullying and physical or psychological negative symptoms: Anxiety and depression as mediators. *Europe's Journal of Psychology*, 15(4), 808–822. https://doi.org/10.5964/ejop.v15i4.1733

Lu, Y., Sun, M., Li, Y., Wu, L., Zhang, X., Wang, J., Huang, Y., & Cao, F. (2023). Association of workplace bullying with suicide ideation and attempt among Chinese nurses during the COVID-19 pandemic. *Journal of Clinical Psychology in Medical Settings*, 30(3), 687–696. https://doi.org/10.1007/s10880-022-09915-3

McTernan, W. P., Dollard, M. F., & LaMontagne, A. D. (2013). Depression in the workplace: An economic cost analysis of depression-related productivity loss attributable to job strain and bullying. *Work & Stress*, 27(4), 321–338.

Mohanty, C. T. (1984). Under Western eyes: Feminist scholarship and colonial discourses. *Boundary*, 2, 333–358.

Namie, G. (2003). Workplace bullying: Escalated incivility. *Ivey business journal*, 68(2), 1–6.

Nauman, S., Malik, S. Z., & Jalil, F. (2019). How workplace bullying jeopardizes employees' life satisfaction: The roles of job anxiety and insomnia. *Frontiers in Psychology*, 10(2292), 1–13. https://www.frontiersin.org/articles/10.3389/fpsyg.2019.02292/full

Nielsen, M. B., Nielsen, G. H., Notelaers, G., & Einarsen, S. (2015). Workplace bullying and suicidal ideation: A 3-wave longitudinal Norwegian study. *American Journal of Public Health*, 105(11), e23–e28. https://doi.org/10.2105/AJPH.2015.302855

Ohene-Nyako, P. (2018). The Heart of the Race: Black women contesting British imperialism and whiteness: Third-World feminist internationalism in Britain in the 1970s-1980s. *Tijdschrift Voor Genderstudies*, 21(3), 249–264.

Patterson, E., Branch, S., Barker, M., & Ramsay, S. (2018). Playing with power: Examinations of types of power used by staff members in workplace bullying – A qualitative interview study. *Qualitative Research in Organizations and Management*, 13(1), 32–52. https://doi.org/10.1108/QROM-10-2016-1441

Pinheiro, J. C. (2022). The Mexican-American War and American Just-War Thinking. *Fides Et Historia*, 54(2), 23–40.

Rodríguez-Muñoz, A., Moreno-Jiménez, B., & Sanz-Vergel, A. I. (2015). Reciprocal relations between workplace bullying, anxiety, and vigor: A two-wave longitudinal study. *Anxiety, Stress, & Coping*, 28(5), 514–530.

Rothbaum, B. O., Astin, M. C., & Marsteller, F. (2005). Prolonged exposure versus eye movement desensitization and reprocessing (EMDR) for PTSD rape victims. *Journal of Traumatic Stress: Official Publication of The International Society for Traumatic Stress Studies, 18*(6), 607–616.

Ruyle, K. (2012, July). Measuring and mitigating cost of employee turnover. Society of Human Resource Management Webcast. http://www.shrm.org/multimedia/webcasts/Documents/12ruyle_2.pdf

Sabbath, E. L., Williams, J. A., Boden, L. I., Tempesti, T., Wagner, G. R., Hopcia, K., Hashimoto, D., & Sorensen, G. (2018). Mental health expenditures. *Journal of Occupational and Environmental Medicine, 60*(8), 737–742. https://doi.org/10.1097/JOM.0000000000001322

Santos, J. F., & Colon-Acevdeo, S. (2020). Puerto Rico becomes first jurisdiction to adopt law against workplace bullying. *The National Law Review.* https://www.natlawreview.com/article/puerto-rico-becomes-first-jurisdiction-to-adopt-law-against-workplace-bullying

Seaver, M. (2015). Employee turnover, what's it costing you? http://michaels-seaver.com/consulting/employee-turnover-what-is-it-costing-you/

Shapiro, F. (2014). The role of eye movement desensitization and reprocessing (EMDR) therapy in medicine: Addressing the psychological and physical symptoms stemming from adverse life experiences. *The Permanente Journal, 18*(1), 71–77.

Stickgold, R. (2002). EMDR: A putative neurobiological mechanism of action. *Journal of Clinical Psychology, 58*(1), 61–75. https://doi.org/10.1002/jclp.1129

Vartia, M. A. (2001). Consequences of workplace bullying with respect to the well-being of its targets and the observers of bullying. *Scandinavian journal of work, environment & health*, 63–69.

Wu, I. H. C., Lyons, B., & Leong, F. T. L. (2015). How racial/ethnic bullying affects rejection sensitivity: The role of social dominance orientation. *Cultural Diversity and Ethnic Minority Psychology, 21*(1), 156–161. https://doi.org/10.1037/a0037930

CHAPTER 12

Afterword: Stop the Math E(race)res

Abstract The afterword reflects on the mis-education that has plausibly contributed to scholars of color to avoid mathematical reasoning. The mis-education that Greeks advanced math erases African and South American mathematical reasoning. Not only does the mis-education, as discussed by Carter G. Woodson, disenfranchise Black and brown scholars, but the mis-education includes replacing Kemet math scholars with Greek math scholars in history. A double intellectual imperialism occurs when students are presumably clean slates devoid of cultural and intellectual grounding [Freire, *Pedagogy of the oppressed*. Herder and Herder (1970)]. Then, the clean slate is infused with falsehoods and mis-education [Woodson, *The Mis-education of the Negro*. First Africa World Press (1933)]. This Afterword chapter adopts the rationale from several Black and African Studies scholars who assign the origins of math reasoning to its proper inception. Consequently, I resist Western authority, which improperly removed Black and brown scholars from mathematical history. Through such resistance, I intend for all scholars, regardless of race, to acknowledge the true origins of math reasoning and knowingly embrace such history to forge mathematical confidence for all scholars. When scholars of color lead quantitative research, they are reasonably sensitive to the need for inclusive samples. Such inclusion and acceptance are needed to advance research that properly reflects diversity.

L. P. Hollis, *Instrumental Social Justice in Higher Education*, https://doi.org/10.1007/978-3-031-49289-1_12

Keywords Miseducation • Freire • Math reasoning • Quantitative research

I have attended several academic educational research conferences with my primary intent to hear about different theoretical applications and processes by which to collect data. While I typically enjoy the application of various theories to data, at these conferences I find very few minoritized scholars who embrace quantitative research methods to study race, gender, and intersectionality. With this idea, I asked several advanced educational researchers if my perception was inaccurate. The deans and department heads I spoke with had the same notion that minoritized scholars shy away from quantitative research methods. By not embracing quantitative methods, minoritized scholars can reinforce the perception that we rarely use quantitative methods.

With this in mind, I developed this mini-book with an opening chapter explaining why minoritized scholars also should use math and statistics. Further, the subsequent chapters review the Cronbach Alpha to validate the instrument and resulting publications and conferences. I intend for this book to motivate social justice scholars to embrace instrument design. The large samples needed for valid quantitative work make such findings more generalizable and applicable to policy development (Polit & Beck, 2010). Further, by explaining my strategies for open-ended survey questions, I show how instrument design can produce robust mixed methods approaches for social justice research.

Workplace bullying is an excellent starting point from which scholars can consider social justice research. The data show that marginalized and disenfranchised populations (minoritized groups, women, immigrants, and the LGBTQA+ community) are disproportionately affected; the outcomes for those targeted by bullies include career interruption and severe health disparities. This book is also a response to several scholars who have requested my instruments, so the surveys in this mini book are presented in the mini-book along with a foundation for creating surveys that address these populations more effectively.

My early academic training was in English literature with an emphasis on African American literature with a second major in Africana Studies. Therefore, my academic world was initially filled with alliterations, metaphors, and imagery. The inception of my academic training came through Alice Walker (2011), Nella Larsen (2001), and Zora Neale Hurston

(1934), Black women writers who used imagery in fiction to capture Black women's struggles in respective historical moments. When I pursued educational policy for my terminal degree, many advising sessions with doctoral committee members included the phrase, "why say in five words what I can say in 25?" as we joked about the need to alter my writing style. Switching from liberal arts writing to a more particular writing in the social sciences challenged me to edit the flowery language from my prose.

I offer this context to say if I could learn survey research, Cronbach's Alpha, multiple regressions, and chi-squared, anyone can. Mastering statistics and validating original survey research gave my research a more comprehensive quality that embraces our ancestors' voices and the predictive power available through some statistical analyses. Regardless of race, gender identity, color, or class, the breadth of statistical procedures like Cronbach's Alpha to validate the findings should not be exclusively deemed as the masters' tools (Lorde, 2001). Too often, the academy explicitly posits that mathematical and statistical reasoning emerges from white culture, as if that hegemonic culture has domain over math and statistics.

From another perspective, Black and brown people often face society's delusion that we possess diminished intellect and ability. For example, the *Presumed Incompetent* series (Harris, 2020; Muhs et al., 2012) highlights Black and brown scholars' voices who have been underestimated and unfairly displaced from some academic circles. Conjointly, sociologists provide the theory that colorism is based on imperialist practices in which privilege is granted to those with light or white skin (Bell, 2019; Burton et al., 2010); society's color prejudice has led many people of color to wrongly perceive themselves as inferior. Empirical research also confirms that the darker the skin tone, the more likely people are targeted at work and in education (Hollis, 2022). Racist, sexist, and discriminatory societal behaviors can pummel people's self-confidence; similarly, Rosario et al. (2021) wrote that colorism erodes confidence and self-esteem.

Erickson and Heit (2015) noted that people need meta-cognition, confidence, and determination to embrace complex processes successfully. An additional residual is that those who overcome or never develop math anxiety, then pursue advanced math college courses, earn 10% more than their counterparts who avoid math (Adkins & Noyes, 2016). In turn, by being subjected to inaccurate assumptions about diminished math reasoning ability, Black and brown folks face the potential problem of garnering lower salaries.

Consequently, Black and brown scholars should resist the false narratives that math belonged to Greeks and other white cultures (James, 2013; Raju, 2017). Identifying colonialism in math education and mounting the necessary resistance that can decolonize science and math, academia can correct the misperception that any scholar might harbor about Black and brown people's math abilities.

> colonialism involved a strategy similar to what was used for racism: For a long string of Western philosophers, Hume (1854), Kant (2011), Hegel (Bernasconi, 2003), and so forth, used the same false history to morally justify racism by asserting the noncreativity of Blacks. (Raju, 2017, p. 257)

The dominant culture misrepresented Black Egypt, also known as Kemet, to assign math proficiency as emerging from Greek culture (Asante & Mazama, 2002; James, 2013; Raju, 2017). In making this point, Raju (2017) references Brodie (2016), who claimed, "Much, though certainly not all, mathematics is the work of dead white men" (para. 2). Such inaccurate positions that infiltrate western mathematical instruction contribute to most students "blindly rel[ying] on Western authority and conflat[ing] it with infallible truth" (Raju, 2017, p. 265). Discounting Black Kemet mathematical foundations while erroneously upholding Greek history as the origin of math manifests as an assumed superiority for white culture while simultaneously colonizing Black mathematical aptitude. The drive to diminish Black folks' ingenuity was so extreme, myths such as the aliens building the Pyramids of Giza (Wilkes, 2023) became a common story. The falsehoods leave minoritized groups toiling under such academic colonization and then believing they have a diminished place in an academic discipline that their ancestors helped to establish.

Analogously, Carter G. Woodson has noted, education has been used to misinform and subordinate Black and brown people (Rashid, 2005). From 1933, Woodson wrote:

> The education of the Negro, then must be carefully directed lest the race may waste time trying to do the impossible. Lead the Negro to believe this and thus control his thinking. If you can thereby determine what he will think, you will not need to worry about what he will do. (p. 192)

Rashid continues by reflecting on what happens to a population of people who have been intellectually subjugated. Further, miseducation erases Black and brown populations from historical accomplishments and compromises that population's agency and self-determination (Karenga, 1997; Rashid, 2005).

I further incorporate Freire's (1970) position from *Pedagogy of the Oppressed* with Woodson's miseducation position. Freire (1970) posits that people are not a blank slate, absent of culture or perspective. However, education often assumes that learners are simply absorbing knowledge, regardless of its legitimacy. The colonization of math, as discussed by Asante and Mazama (2002), James (2013), and Raju (2017), not only assumes students are blank slates, but confirms that the colonists' approach also creates the blank-slate-learner by denying them information regarding cultural origins of mathematical reasoning. By e(race)ing the Black Egyptian contribution, that is removing race, Black and brown communities are left unaware of their ancestors' intellect or ingenuity. In short, the colonists wipe the slate clean, manipulate the history, then feed it back to Black and brown communities, yet reframed the history as the colonists' invention.

To disrupt the intellectual vulture who takes someone else's accomplishments and repositions the accomplishments as their own, educators should discourage the historical intellectual erasure and instead present a more culturally accurate depiction of mathematical reasoning and its origins. Such erasures cause detriment to all when anyone in society is disenfranchised, then rendered psychologically dispossessed without a tether to ancestral knowledge and intellectual history. At times, the community continues looking for what was erased so the proper historical and intellectual position is reinstated. While imperialist manipulation of history hurts Kemet descendants who were misled to believing Greeks had superior reasoning, the more egregious contention is society's misrepresentation of Kemet's innovative brain power. The whole society suffers when any member of society is denied its authentic positionality.

Hence, the goal of this book on social justice instrument development and validation through Cronbach Alpha is congruent with Raju's (2017) recommendation that the academy needs to deconstruct racially motivated philosophy about math and pivot to teach an accurate history of math reasoning. Further, the educational field needs more scholars to incorporate communities of color into research methods such as mixed methods and predictive models. Researchers across disciplines comment that Black and brown people are often missing from data sets. For example, Cho (2022) opines that students regarding math anxiety include samples in which Black and brown underrepresented minorities are largely absent. Like Cho (2022), many may consider research devoid of Black and brown voices incomplete or inaccurate. The same conclusion applies to academic and public policies devised without consideration for a range of communities, not just the ruling and privileged class.

The intersection of homogenous data and math anxiety for minoritized researchers can create a research vacuum absent of diversity. Though qualitative research is good to bring forward voices from disenfranchised populations, quantitative research can produce more generalizable findings when inclusive of race-balanced and gender-balanced samples (Polit & Beck, 2010). Whether one is studying workplace bullying, health disparities, employment discrimination, elder abuse, or nutrition, such studies need insight from a diverse sample. One way to cultivate more inclusive research is to educate students about the true origins of math and statistics. Logical reasoning appeared well before Muslims advanced Aristotle's ideas during the Crusades, approximately 1500 years after Aristotle's death (James, 2013; Raju, 2017). Subsequently, math, statistics, and other advanced reasoning belong to all students, not just those who benefit from colonized math, false narratives, and the related fallacy that minoritized people lack the ability for advanced mathematical and statistical computation.

REFERENCES

Adkins, M., & Noyes, A. (2016). Reassessing the economic value of advanced level mathematics. *British Educational Research Journal, 42*(1), 93–116. https://doi.org/10.1002/berj.3219

Asante, M., & Mazama, A. (2002). *Egypt versus Greece and the American academy.* African American Image.

Bell, J. F. (2019). Confronting colorism: Interracial abolition and the consequences of complexion. *Journal of the Early Republic., 39*(2), 239–266.

Bernasconi, R. (2003). Hegel's racism. *Radical Philosophy, 119,* 35–37.

Brodie, K. (2016, August). Yes, mathematics can be decolonised. Here's how to begin. *The Conversation.* https://theconversation.com/yes-mathematics-can-be-decolonised-heres-how-to-begin-65963

Burton, L. M., Bonilla-Silva, E., Ray, V., Buckelew, R., & Hordge Freeman, E. (2010). Critical race theories, colorism, and the decade's research on families of color. *Journal of Marriage and Family, 72*(3), 440–459.

Cho, K. W. (2022). Measuring math anxiety among predominantly underrepresented minority undergraduates using the abbreviated math anxiety scale. *Journal of Psychoeducational Assessment, 40*(3), 416–429. https://doi.org/10.1177/07342829211063286

Erickson, S., & Heit, E. (2015). Metacognition and confidence: Comparing math to other academic subjects. *Frontiers in Psychology, 6,* 742. https://doi.org/10.3389/fpsyg.2015.00742

Freire, P. (1970). *Pedagogy of the oppressed.* Herder and Herder.

Harris, A. P. (2020). *Presumed incompetent II: Race, class, power, and resistance of women in academia.* University Press of Colorado.

Hollis, L. P. (2022). Brown and Bullied Around: The Relationship between Colorism and Workplace Bullying for African Americans/Blacks. In L. P. Hollis (Ed.), *Black women, intersectionality and workplace bullying: Intersecting Distress.* Routledge.

Hume, D. (1854). *The philosophical works of David Hume.* Little, Brown.

Hurston, Z. N. (1934). Characteristics of Negro expression. *African American Literary Theory: A Reader,* 31–44.

James, G. G. (2013). *Stolen legacy.* Simon and Schuster.

Kant, I. (2011). *Observations on the feeling of the beautiful and the sublime and other writings.* Cambridge University.

Karenga, M. (1997). *Kawaida theory: A communication African philosophy.* University of Sankore Press.

Larsen, N. (2001). *The complete fiction of Nella Larsen: Passing, quicksand, and the stories.* Anchor.

Lorde, A. (2001). *The master's tools.* Richardson, Taylor, & Whittier (Eds.). Feminist Frontiers V. New York: McGraw-Hill.

Muhs, G. G., Niemann, Y. F., González, C. G., & Harris, A. P. (Eds.). (2012). *Presumed incompetent: The intersections of race and class for women in academia.* University Press of Colorado.

Polit, D. F., & Beck, C. T. (2010). Generalization in quantitative and qualitative research: Myths and strategies. *International Journal of Nursing Studies, 47*(11), 1451–1458.

Raju, C. K. (2017). Black thoughts matter: Decolonized math, academic censorship, and the "Pythagorean" proposition. *Journal of Black Studies, 48*(3), 256–278. https://doi.org/10.1177/0021934716688311

Rashid, K. (2005). Slavery of the mind: Carter G. Woodson and Jacob H. Carruthers-intergenerational discourse on African education and social change. *Western Journal of Black Studies, 29*(1). 542-546.

Rosario, R. J., Minor, I., & Rogers, L. O. (2021). "Oh, you're pretty for a dark-skinned girl": Black adolescent girls' identities and resistance to colorism. *Journal of Adolescent Research, 36*(5), 501–534.

Walker, A. (2011). *The color purple*. Open Road Media.

Wilkes, J. (2023). Were the pyramids built by aliens? The real history that debunks the conspiracy. *History Extra. The official website for BBC History Magazine and BBC History Revealed*. https://www.historyextra.com/period/ancient-egypt/were-pyramids-built-by-aliens-conspiracy-real-history-facts/

Woodson, C. G. (1933). *The Mis-education of the Negro*. First Africa World Press.

INDEX

© The Author(s), under exclusive license to Springer Nature
Switzerland AG 2024
L. P. Hollis, *Instrumental Social Justice in Higher Education*,
https://doi.org/10.1007/978-3-031-49289-1

GPSR Compliance

The European Union's (EU) General Product Safety Regulation (GPSR) is a set of rules that requires consumer products to be safe and our obligations to ensure this.

If you have any concerns about our products, you can contact us on ProductSafety@springernature.com

In case Publisher is established outside the EU, the EU authorized representative is:

Springer Nature Customer Service Center GmbH
Europaplatz 3
69115 Heidelberg, Germany

The manufacturer's authorised representative in the EU is Springer
Nature Customer Service Centre GmbH, Europaplatz 3, 69115 Heidelberg,
Germany. If you have any concerns regarding our products, please
contact ProductSafety@springernature.com

Printed and bound by CPI Group (UK) Ltd, Croydon, CR0 4YY

24/04/2026
02096315-0017